The Questions of
Christian Faith

D1516071

what
to
believe?

CARL E. KRIEG

WHAT TO BELIEVE?

WHAT TO BELIEVE?

The Questions of Christian Faith

CARL E. KRIEG

FORTRESS PRESS   Philadelphia

Library of Congress Catalog Card Number 74-80415

ISBN 0-8006-1085-7

4264C74   Printed in the United States of America   1-1085

CONTENTS

89502

CONTENTS

INTRODUCTION

Too often in society we find an almost impassable gulf between the thought-world of the professional and that of the non-professional. To a certain extent this lack of communication—and of the ability to communicate—is acceptable and necessary. The man-in-the-street need not know the physics and technology involved in sending a man to the moon. Indeed, without years of education he could not know. This is not the case, however, with theology. The question of the relationship between God and man is not a topic reserved for the ivy walls of the academic world. This question, which is the subject of theology, is not and must not be divorced from the everyday affairs of human life. Unfortunately, it is the case all too often that this divorce exists.

This book is an attempt to bridge the gap between the professional theologian and anyone who cares to ask the question of God. There is a conscious effort to avoid technical jargon as much as possible and, where possible, to exemplify a theological concept rather than merely to state it. Though the issues are both subtle and complex, clarity and simplicity have been the goal; but without, I hope, sacrificing carefulness or sophistication.

Many introductions to Christian belief present the material with a sort of "here it is" attitude: Here is what Christians believe. Books written with such an attitude may be informative but are often not very helpful. Our approach here is different. Like it or not, Christian thought is shot through with problems and riddles which admit of no easy answer. Our chapter titles end with a question mark, not a period. The attitude expressed in these pages is, therefore, not that of "here is what you have to believe to qualify for Christian status." Instead, we propose a journey through the *questions* of theology, and not simply through the answers. Problems, of course, suggest answers, and much of the material herein presented will involve answers. But here again the answers themselves will be presented as problematic.

Various topics are considered. The order of the chapters could very well have been otherwise. There is no progression of thought that requires the chapters to be read in sequence. In the same vein, there is no conscious effort to defend a particular type of theology. I am not arguing for one type of answer as opposed to another. Yet, the reader will feel, quite rightly, that on occasion the author is inclined more to one position than another. There is no need for apologies on this point; a purely disinterested presentation would be a bore. Generally, the chapters will begin with a problem, followed by various answers which will betray the author's own inclination, if any.

WHAT TO BELIEVE?

1

WHY DO SOME PEOPLE BELIEVE IN GOD?

Lots of people in the world use the word "god" or its equivalent. Of course, the word is used in various contexts and with different intentions. The sentence: "I believe in God," uses the word quite differently than does the sentence: "God damn it"—a sentence evoked when, for example, the hammer hits your finger instead of the nail. If we propose to ask why some people talk about God, we have in mind those persons who believe in God, who believe that God exists. This, then, is our first question: Given the fact that some people have some kind of faith in God—Why? Why do people believe in God?

There are a variety of answers to the question, but generally they fall into two categories. On the one hand, it is argued that God really exists, that people know him, and therefore they believe in and talk about him. The second approach is quite the opposite, asserting that faith in God is just some kind of delusion, a crutch that people lean on, a Big-Friend-in-the-Sky that man invents. There are some specific theories which illustrate this second approach.

Ludwig Feuerbach, nineteenth-century philosopher, suggested a simple explanation for religious belief. According to him, all men want to have certain basic characteristics. Men want to be strong, to have knowledge, to be totally free and loving. These desires they push to the limit. Man really wants to be omnipotent: to have all power; to be omniscient: to have all knowledge. There is an ideal, a perfect man, that we can all think about. The ideal, however, doesn't live on earth. No man on this planet has all power or all knowledge. Men are finite, they're imperfect, they die. So, on the one hand, human beings have in their minds the idea of the perfect man. On the other hand, the facts of life are that nobody achieves this perfect state. In the face of this contradiction, our minds play a simple trick on us: we invent a God who is everything we want to be but can't be. I may not be omnipotent, but God is. I may not live forever, but God does. I may not know everything, but God does. God is my wish-fulfillment. As Feuerbach puts it, "If birds had a god, he would be a perfect winged creature." The writer of Genesis says that man was created in God's image. Actually, according to Feuerbach, the reverse occurs: man creates God in his—man's—own image.

The trouble is that man starts to get lazy; he begins to wait for God to do things. "I should help to stop this war. But God is stronger; I'll let him do it." "I should fight pollution. But God wouldn't let his creation rot away; he'll do something." The man who believes in God, says Feuerbach, begins to forget his responsibility as a human being, and this is self-destructive. For this reason Feuerbach was antireligious. We should note that he was an atheist out of the best possible motive—that of making man more responsible, more loving, more human.

Why do people talk about God? Feuerbach's answer is that man wants to be perfect but can't be. So he invents a God who is perfect. God-talk is really man-talk. When man says something about God, he is really *only* saying something about himself and what he wants to be like.

Another theory on the origin of religion offers a somewhat different analysis. Like Feuerbach's, this view too sees God as a mere illusion of men's minds; but the theories of the origin of the illusion are different. One is based on man's relationship to nature. Nature is hard and cruel, and in his fear of impersonal nature, man humanizes the forces of nature. The storm, the mountain, the tree, are viewed as animated by a spirit, a living, personal force. Having invented spirits which inhabit nature, man now invents ways and means to deal with these spirits. Sacrifice, for example, is a desire to appease the wrath of the gods. As time passes and man matures, the many gods coalesce into one god: the god of the mountain is seen to be the same as the god of the tree, the river, etc. Ultimately, therefore, a single god is created by man, a god whom man both fears and needs, just as he both fears and needs nature. This god does not exist in reality outside man's imagination; he is merely an invention of the human mind.

A related theory of Sigmund Freud on the origin of religion is especially intriguing. Freud posited a primitive horde of men that lived "in the beginning." In this horde a jealous father kept all the females for himself. The sons, frustrated by the father's selfishness, conspired to take the life of the father. This they did, all equally participating in the act of murder. But there continued in them a sense of awe and love for the deceased father, combined with fear and hatred. This intense longing for the father gave rise to the father-ideal which in turn led to the creation of god-the-father. God, therefore, is a creation of the guilty conscience, modelled after the primeval father, a father simultaneously loved, feared, needed, and hated. This psychological process, according to Freud, goes on in the mind of every little boy who competes with the father for mommy's love and attention. Belief in God the Father is a consequence of the Oedipal neurosis. To those who pray "Our Father, who art in heaven, . . ." this theory should be at least disturbing.

There is also what can be described as a politico-economic reason why people believe in God. Such a theory was formulated by Karl Marx in the late nineteenth century. Generalizing this theory, we may put it thus: In any society, economic power practically determines everything else. Economic power generates political power: people with money will exercise great influence over the operations of the state. In addition to this, with economico-political power goes the ability to infiltrate the thought-levels of society, including the moral and religious. In a very real way wealth gives its holder the power to determine the total outlook of a culture. Applying this analysis to religion, we come up with the following results. The poor are told: "Obey the authorities, for the authorities represent God. To rebel would be to go against God. If you are a poor worker, or a slave, it is because God in His providence put you there. You don't want to be contrary to God's will, do you? And remember, the days of your life on earth are not that important. You will go to heaven, you know, provided you are content with your lot." And so on. Consciously or not, the rich create a God who both justifies and supports the power they wield. This God is foisted upon the poor, who in turn religiously accept their fate.

Finally, we may note that many people who believe in God actually recognize and admit that this God is nothing but a figment of their imagination. People become lonely and depressed, and discover that belief in God makes them "feel better." This God is recognized as a crutch, an escape, but is still accepted.

Why do men believe in God? We have looked at one type of answer, illustrated by a number of theories. According to this approach, people believe in God because of psychological, economic, or sociological reasons—but not because he exists independently in reality. Common to all these theories is the fundamental notion that God is a creation of the human mind, a fantasy with no existence in and of himself.

There is, however, another answer to the question. There is the possibility that God does in fact exist, that he is not merely a figment of man's imagination. Further, that people believe in this God because he has made himself known to them. Christian theology opts for this possibility.

Further elaboration is unnecessary. The two options are quite clear. We are not asking why some believe in God and others don't, but why those who do, do. One possibility is self-delusion; the other is that God in fact exists. The unfortunate truth seems to be that neither of the answers can be proven. This means that everyone who believes in God should be painfully aware of the possibility that he has created his own god, a god who is fictional. Similarly, one who believes he has conclusively explained in a natural way that belief is delusion, should admit that such matters are incapable of proof.

2

HOW IS CHRISTIANITY RELATED TO OTHER RELIGIONS?

If it is true that some people talk about God, it is also true that they talk about him in various ways. Within the Christian camp there are Catholics, Eastern Orthodox, and Protestants, not to mention the many sects and denominations. Alongside this Christian religion are the many other religions of man, e.g., Buddhism, Hinduism, and Islam. To this may be added the infinite variety of smaller and less formal religions such as Baalism, sun-worship, Baha'i.

The fact that there is a variety of religions raises a simple but basic question: Is there any religion which may be called "true," as opposed to all others which would be "false"? Christians have always believed that their God and their faith were true, and that the gods of other religions were false idols, worshipped by pagans. In recent years, however, increased knowledge of other peoples, better communication, and more sensitive understanding have led many people to be more humble in claiming the absolute truth for their own faith. In many ways the pendulum has swung completely from one position to another. As we said, Christians have traditionally viewed their religion as the only true religion. This attitude is probably still prevalent among church people today. But conversation with people who call themselves Christian indicates a new perspective: the right to believe what one wants, and the right to claim one's faith is true. That is, the emerging mood is that there is no one true religion, but that all religions are true for those who profess them.

This fact of the variety of religious beliefs raises some difficult questions for Christian theology. Since we are attempting to understand the Christian faith, let us make the following assumptions: 1) that God exists in reality, and 2) this God has revealed himself in Jesus Christ. Given this basic Christian faith, there are at least three attitudes that one might take with respect to other religions.

One could stick with the orthodox view that the Christian position alone is true and accurate. There is but one God, a Triune God, and this God has saved men in some unique way through Jesus Christ. Jesus Christ. Jesus Christ is the Only Son of God, and salvation comes only through faith in him. Such a position might be termed one of uncompromising absolutism.

It is usually on the basis of such a position that the church has sent missionaries to foreign lands. Especially in the last century, but also today, many institutional churches believe it is incumbent upon them to "carry the gospel" to the distant corners of the globe which have never heard the good news of Jesus. The underlying assumption of this traditionally conceived missionary enterprise is that the Christian religion is alone true, and that salvation depends on one's acceptance of Jesus as Savior.

A second alternative would be that of absolute relativism. In this view, Christians would have every right to believe that their God saved *them* through Jesus, and that the requirement for people in *their* community is faith in the God revealed in Christ. In other words, for Christians, Christianity is true, but not necessarily for Moslems. For the Moslems, Allah is God, and Allah has spoken through his prophet, Mohammed. For Moslems, the Moslem religion is true. Matters of faith are only true relative to the community which shares that faith. The attitude of the Christian faith would be "confessional." That is, Christians could say: "We believe that God was saving the world in Christ Jesus. We believe this is so, and we invite you to consider and perhaps share this belief. But if you choose to remain Moslem, that too is right and proper." If this position is *absolutely* relative, one would have to conclude that there may be, in reality, a number of gods and therefore a number of valid and true religions.

Most relativists are not absolutist, however. Most would balk at the suggestion of there being a number of gods. Instead, they would assume a sort of modified relativism, asserting that there is *one* God who has related himself to man in a *variety* of ways. Moses, Mohammed, Buddha, and Jesus are all prophets of this one God who has sent a number of messengers to man. Buddhists know and worship this God in the way of Buddha; Christians know and worship this one God in the way of Jesus. Such a modified relativism is actually a very common position. Many people think there is one God who is worshipped by men in many different ways. Such a view is recognized as respectable because it is tolerant of other people's opinions.

For the Christian, each of these positions is problematic. The first position, total absolutism, faces the problem of what to think about all the people who never, so to speak, hear the good news about Jesus. It is probable that a majority of the world's population never hears the Christian gospel. Does this mean they are doomed to eternal destruction? Even those who do hear the gospel often find that the Christian religion is totally alien to their indigenous culture and mentality, and therefore reject all Christian God-talk. Are they, too, eternally doomed?

The second position has equally serious difficulties. If all matters of faith are totally relative and there is a plurality of gods, does it make sense to place total trust in any one such god? Why bother with a god if he is not the Creator and Sustainer of the Universe? No doubt, faith in a limited deity among deities was prevalent in man's earlier stages of development. Perhaps such a faith is possible also today. But such a stand, besides having no basis on which to criticize the demonic, would require a total reinterpretation of what Christianity is all about.

This last comment holds true also for the third position. In a modified relativism, the importance traditionally assigned to Jesus Christ would have to be totally reevaluated. Essential to the gospel is the view that Christ and Christ alone is able to reconcile men to God and to one another. If, now, Jesus is to be placed on equal footing with men such as Moses and Buddha, then the Christian must think anew the meaning of the Trinity, the Crucifixion, and everything related thereto.

There is, however, a fourth alternative which is worthy of consideration. In this view, consistent with biblical tradition, God is seen as one God who in Christ reconciled men unto himself. That is, Christ is confessed as the only mediator between God and man. Personal faith in this Christ, however, may not be required for inclusion in this reconciliation. Perhaps Buddha, for example, is a representative of Christ, so that Christ "uses" Buddha to create love and responsibility among men—love and responsibility which is made possible because of what Christ did. This position would be summed up in the following statements: 1) Reconciliation and love between man and man, and man and God, is made possible because of what Jesus Christ did for man. 2) And yet, a person need not believe in Jesus Christ in order to be reconciled and loving. If a label were required, such a position might be called one of modified absolutism.

At any rate, however one solves the question in his own mind, it is clear that the variety of religions presents a problem for Christian theology. As with most theological matters, we will probably never arrive at an answer which is completely satisfactory. In the meantime, each person should be both sufficiently committed and open-minded to say: "This is how I see it. What do you think?"

3

HOW DO WE ANSWER
OUR QUESTIONS?

When a person has a difference of opinion with his neighbor about the boundary separating their land, they go to court to settle the fight. If two students disagree as to the right answer on an examination question, they pick up their papers, and the professor, rightly or wrongly, has settled the issue. If you are curious as to when Lincoln was born, the answer is readily available. But suppose you and your roommate argue about God—where or to whom can you go to settle the matter? In other words, who or what has the *authority* to settle theological questions? Inasmuch as we are attempting to understand Christian theology, this question will be considered as a question for the Christian faith.

If you were a Protestant about three hundred years ago, the answer was easy. It was good, orthodox Protestant belief that the sole authority was the Bible. Not only did the Bible supply an absolute answer to every theological question, but everything in the Bible, pertaining to the faith or not, was considered absolutely true. Biblical pronouncements on geography, medicine, history, and politics were taken as sacred truth. Everything in Holy Scripture was asserted to be infallibly true.

The doctrine of the infallibility of Scripture contains certain basic ideas which should be delineated. To begin with, infallibility means inerrancy: every word, sentence, comma, and period in the original languages are believed to have directly proceeded from the mouth of God. The writers of Scripture are seen as receivers of dictation—the Holy Spirit came down and either whispered the words in their ears, or guided their hand in writing, or both. The Bible is thus seen as a sort of frisbee which God dropped down from heaven, with a thunderous: "Here it is; take it or leave it."

As such a deposit of perfect information, the literal meaning of Scripture must be accepted. The applications are numerous. If the Bible said the world was created in seven days, so it was. And the first five books of the Old Testament were written by Moses. And there was a garden called Eden, inhabited by Adam and Eve. And Jesus performed miracles, and the book of Daniel tells us when the world will end (if only we could decipher the message). Since the Word of God is contained in Scripture, to believe in God means to "believe in the Bible," as inerrant. Contradiction in the Bible is only apparent, for with proper inspiration from the Holy Spirit one will be able to reconcile all disparity.

With the rise of scientific investigation and biblical scholarship, the simple acceptance of the orthodox view was bound to come under attack. For the most part, the Bible views the world as a sort of three-decker sandwich. Heaven is on top, hell is on the bottom, with the world of men in between. In this worldview, heaven is "up," and it makes sense to say that Jesus came down to be man, that he descended into hell, then rose, and ascended into heaven, and in the future will descend upon the clouds. But now we know that the earth is spherical, or pear-shaped, or banana-shaped (it seems to change every year)—at any rate we do know at least that it is not flat. Up for a Chinaman is down for an American. Does it any longer make sense to speak of Christ later descending upon the clouds? If one happens to be on the wrong side of the world, the whole show will be missed when Jesus comes again!

Not only did the Bible portray a three-decker universe but the middle slice—earth—could be invaded periodically by supernatural visitors from without. God from above and the Devil from below were frequently barging in and performing miracles or tormenting men. (Remember Job.) But now science provides us with alternative explanations of "miraculous" events. Lightning is not a bolt thrown by an angry god, but a discharge of static electricity. Persons are not possessed by demons, but are analyzed as neurotic or psychotic. God did not send a flood, the icecaps melted. has enabled us to de-spiritualize the world so we now have a secular outlook. This development meant, of course, that many of the events described by the Bible could no longer be accepted as literally true.

Studies of other religions and other cultures showed that the themes of many biblical stories were also present in other sacred scriptures. The Old Testament story of Elijah giving to a woman a pot of porridge which never emptied, for example, is a common tale in folklore. The impact of this broadened awareness raised further questions about the uniqueness of the Bible itself, and therefore its claim to inerrancy.

It was inevitable that scientific literary criticism would ultimately be applied to the Bible itself. When scholars examined the original manuscripts and took a critical position toward Scripture, the effect was to cast further doubt on the doctrine of absolute inerrancy. Literary and historical analysis showed that the first five books of the Old Testament were not written by Moses at all, but instead were a composite of at least four different sources—and written over a period of hundreds of years. A simple illustration lies in a comparison of Genesis 1 and 2. In one chapter man is created first, in the other man is created last. The two chapters use different Hebrew names for God. Conclusion? They were written by different authors. Judges and Joshua both describe the Hebrew invasion of Palestine. According to Joshua, the invasion was accomplished quickly, whereas Judges describes the invasion as a painful, prolonged process. Conclusion?

The implications are varied. Clearly, the Bible contradicts itself on matters of fact; in this case, history. A more significant result, however, was to raise the question concerning the intent of the biblical writers. Would they consciously lie? Why do accounts differ? One possibility, accepted by many, is that much of the biblical material was never intended to be taken literally. That is, perhaps the prophets and apostles wrote what we might call a story with a message, a story in which the actual wording was not intended to be taken literally. If this is true, then clearly what we need to do today is to dig out the meaning of the material, and not even pretend to believe in inerrancy.

But suppose that some of the biblical material *was* intended by the author to be taken literally. Suppose the author of Genesis 1 *did* in fact believe that the world was created in seven days. The question then becomes: Can we today accept that? The answer of many, in the face of geological and biological evidence, is: Certainly not! What do we do then with these Bible stories— throw them away as irrelevant? Some do that. Others reject the literal wording and look for "the message" that applies and is acceptable to us today.

In other words, critical examination of the Bible showed that many biblical stories either were not intended to be taken literally or could not be taken literally. Further, it was generally agreed that biblical writers were not so much interested in matters of geography and history as they were in matters of faith and ethics. Consider an illustration.

Moses, we are told, went up to the top of Mt. Sinai and received directly from God two tablets inscribed with ten commandments. Perhaps the authors intended the story to be taken literally. In that case, modern Christians informed by science would look for the *meaning* of the story. For example: These laws are good for society and we believe that somehow God wants us to live after this fashion. But, then, maybe that's what the Hebrew authors themselves intended. Having taken over Palestine, they naturally developed a system of law. Perhaps they took customs from the several tribes, borrowed legal codes from neighboring peoples, and molded all of these into the "Ten Commandments." Although fully aware of just how these laws were assembled, perhaps the Hebrews believed that in some way God had guided the process, thereby "giving" them the Law. This interpretation of the Moses story makes sense even for us today.

Illustrative material is endless. The point is that the doctrine of biblical inerrancy is all but eroded away in the minds of many modern Christians. Instead of seeing the Bible as an infallible handbook for all sorts of disciplines, people look for its meaning. And the meaning is seen as basically limited to matters of faith and ethics, i.e., what to believe and how to live. And even here, what the Bible says is not taken as absolutely authoritative. Rather, the authority of Scripture is now seen by many as a partner in dialogue, offering advice but not definitive answers. "This is the way that some people thought about this matter two thousand years ago. We must take it into consideration, but it is not absolutely binding upon us." When Saint Paul says that in church women are to keep their mouths shut and cover their heads and be obedient to their husbands, his words are taken under advisement and not proclaimed as the will of a male, chauvinistic God!

This capacity of the Bible as advisor or partner in dialogue is obviously at odds with the orthodox position. The basis for this view is that God is believed to have acted in some special ways during biblical times. People were caught up in what was happening, and began to have faith in this God—and also to reflect upon their encounter with him. Much of this reflection was preserved orally and in manuscript. The Scriptures, therefore, are the words of persons who believed that God was acting in special ways, who sought to describe this activity, and who related as well as possible the response of the people concerned. In this view the Bible is neither a divine monologue nor a common piece of literature. It is, instead, written by men of faith who had faith in the God to whom they witness. As an authority, therefore, it is certainly weighty and significant. But its authority is not that of an inerrant oracle.

Old orthodox Protestantism held the Bible to be infallibly

authoritative on everything. Modern Protestantism holds it authoritative in an *advisory* fashion only on matters of *faith* and *ethics*. But what happens when two individuals read the same passage in the Bible and disagree as to its meaning? Consider an example. We are both Christians, and we've just read about Jesus turning water into wine. You think he really did perform a miracle; I don't. How do we settle our argument?

At this point an orthodox Christian will say "Aha! See what confusion develops when the absolute authority of Scripture is denied!" But the same dilemma can happen to two parties who accept the Bible as fully authoritative. Take Luther and his Catholic opponents. Both sides read Saint Paul's comments on justification—but each interpreted them differently. How did Luther become so bold as to assume that his interpretation alone was correct? We should remember in this connection that Luther was not eager to break away from Rome; he questioned his act just as we can. What was his authority for breaking away? Was it Scripture? Not solely, for Rome also appealed to Scripture. In the final analysis, it was Luther himself, his own conscience, which for him operated as the final judge.

Liberal or not, Christians who turn to the Bible for answers find themselves of necessity interpreting the Bible. Who then interprets? Why, *I* do, of course! Biblicist or not, we must admit that there are at least two sources of authority: the Bible, and our own minds.

But we can push one step further. When you have a problem or a question, what do you do? It is a natural phenomenon that in times of stress or confusion, a person turns to others for advice and comfort. If your sweetheart is giving you a hard time, you talk it over with your best friend. The same thing happens within the church, again and again. When there is confusion, individuals turn not only to the Bible and to their own best judgment, they turn to one another. The history of the early church is the history of councils, of Christians getting together to hammer out answers to questions. In many churches today, especially the Catholic church, tradition represents an authoritative voice. And what is tradition but the advice of the ages, the living voice of the past. The simple question: What do *you* think? represents a profound human interdependency.

Turning to others for advice has reached its epitome in the Roman doctrine of papal infallibility. Here the voice of the fellowman is taken as absolute. But proclamations of the pope are hardly the sort of neighborly comfort which we all seek. To some Protestant theologians it seems that the Catholic papacy destroys the very co-humanity it seeks to serve. The fundamental problem lies in the understanding of the church. Suppose that instead of an authoritative hierarchy, culminating in the pope, the church was a fellowship of believers, bound together in democratic fashion. When a question arose, you could turn to the fellowship to discuss the matter, receiving their advice and opinion. In this way, biblical authority and personal interpretation can be tempered by a third force: communal opinion.

Taking these three together seems to represent a valid approach to the problem of authority. In asking a question about what to believe or what to do, it makes good sense to examine biblical evidence. The Bible, however, must be interpreted and made applicable in your own life. In so interpreting and applying, you turn to others in the community in order to share the benefits of their knowledge and experience. Authority, therefore, is threefold: biblical, personal, communal.

This means that there is no easy answer as to what is right and what is wrong. Suppose, for example, that a person believes something about Jesus Christ which is neither biblical nor supported by tradition. Searching the Scriptures, he finds passages which may be interpreted as supporting this position, but no one else in the community of faith agrees with his idea. What then? Is this person no longer a Christian? Is everyone else wrong? There is no easy solution. In fact, the history of the early church indicates that constant struggle between conflicting opinions characterized the first centuries of the Christian faith.

There was and there is no original body of doctrine which must be believed if one is to be a Christian. What the church has come to accept as basic is the product of years and years of often bitter debate. A heretic was a heretic only because he lost the argument! Had he won, his position would have become orthodox. The development of Christian dogma, therefore, was a rather dynamic process. Decisions were often made at large councils, where political intrigue combined with theological incompetence. This resulted in certain ideas about God and man which we today accept as orthodox. But, in principle, nothing is absolute. The only reason we have certain basic creeds is because the church agreed upon these creeds as incorporating the essence of the Christian faith. Consequently, it is generally felt that to be a Christian, one must adhere to at least those beliefs presented in the creeds. And yet it must be remembered that the creeds represent only the opinion of the ruling majority, an opinion entrenched through tradition. The assumption of the church, however, is that somehow God was guiding the decision-making process so that the creeds do, in fact, represent the truth.

We today think of ourselves as enlightened, tolerant persons. We refuse to call anyone a heretic; we refuse to kick anyone out of the fellowship of faith. If, therefore, a person were to arise with a new idea which stood clearly outside the pale of Christian faith as defined by the Scriptures and the church, he could probably continue in his "heretical" belief as long as he was not, shall we say, a Sunday School teacher! How such a person is to think of himself and how others are to think of him is an open question. What is acceptable and what is not is an open question. The least one can say is that orthodox persons ought to listen attentively to what the free-thinker is saying, and vice-versa. For it is precisely this sort of dialogue, today as two thousand years ago, which exhibits the vitality of Christian thought. Let no one, therefore, be so foolish as to think he can settle a debate with: The Bible says, or Luther says, or the pope says. Truth is much freer than that.

4

HOW DOES GOD
MAKE HIMSELF KNOWN?

In chapter 1 it was explained that Christians believe that their belief in God is not a big illusion. Rather, they believe that God does in fact exist and that he has made himself known to man. Given this assumption, it becomes necessary to ask about the manner in which God makes himself known. This is the problem of revelation. "To reveal" means to make known, so that the Christian doctrine of revelation represents an attempt to describe the ways that God makes himself known.

Most theologians talk about revelation in two ways. We need to identify these two types of revelation and then see how they are related. First, there is natural revelation. This phrase encompasses two basic ideas. On the one hand, it is intended to convey the thought that God is present everywhere in the world around us. That is, God makes himself known to man in a variety of natural means and experiences which are available to all men. For example, we've all read or heard accounts of someone's sense of the divine as he stood in awe of the majesty and grandeur of nature, such as in a sunset. Standing atop a high mountain and gazing across the horizon, or staring in wonder at the starry skies above—such experiences might be occasions for man to become aware of the presence of God. Certain chords are struck when one is confronted with death, just as other chords are struck when one witnesses the miracle of birth. In such experiences, where the depths of human existence are sounded, there is again the occasion for man to become cognizant of the divine reality. The list of such experience is endless. The point is that God's presence is universally present in natural experience. This presence is natural, it is universal, it is "general."

The concept of natural (universal, general) revelation implies secondly that, if he tries, man can discover this presence of God in the world about him. The assumption is that each and every human being has the ability to contemplate himself and his world, and in so doing will become aware of God. This presupposition is common to all of man's searches for God. Throughout his history man has sought the pathway to God, assuming of course, that the search would be fruitful. The so-called proofs for the existence of God are indicative of man's presupposition that he could "arrive at" God if only his proof was sufficiently irrefutable. Although few today follow the rational path in search of God, the search itself is very much a part of our contemporary scene. The hallucinogenic effect of drugs is believed by some to bring a person to the edge of another "zone," a zone which represents the One, the All, Truth and God. In a less bizarre key, but much more widespread, students all over the country are comparing religions. They are shopping around, looking for the one that will bring them to God. Books have been written on all of these phenomena; what concerns us here are two assumptions common to all these searches for God: that God is "there," and that man can find Him if he only tries hard enough. These two assumptions comprise the concept which Christian theology calls "natural revelation".

Secondly, however, Christians also speak of another manner in which God makes himself known, the way of special revelation. The phrase means exactly what it says. In contrast to a natural revelation which is "there" for everybody, special revelation pertains to events which happen at a specific time and place to specific people and are initiated by God, not man. God made himself known to Abraham. That is special revelation. On a larger scale, God dealt with the people of Israel in a way unique to them, a way in which he dealt with no other people. That, too, is special. For Christians, though, the epitome of special revelation is Jesus Christ. It is believed that the life and death of Jesus are par excellence the revelation of God in the flesh of a particular, special human being.

It is obvious that natural revelation is quite different from special revelation. A divine presence open to all contrasts with one open to only a few. A divine presence for which man can search is quite different from a divine manifestation which only God can initiate. This difference between the two manners of revelation has raised a basic question in the minds of theologians, namely, How are they to be related? What is the relationship between natural and special revelation?

As might be expected, there are generally two different kinds of answers to the question, one positive, the other negative. Roman Catholic theology in particular, but also many Protestant theologians, believe that there is a positive and fruitful relationship between the two types of revelation. According to this view, natural revelation lays the groundwork for the special acts of God's revelation. It is seen as prerequisite to special revelation. Just as you recognize Uncle Charlie when he knocks on the door because of previous acquaintance, so too, it is felt, special acts of revelation are recognized because of our previous acquaintance with God in natural experience. The reverse is also true. Just as the visit from Uncle Charlie reinforces our vision of who he is and what he's like, so too, special revelation is seen as eliciting and reaffirming the knowledge of God which man has naturally. In this view, then, there is a positive relationship between the two: natural revelation is weaker or more faint, but it is necessary in order that God's presence in Jesus Christ might be recognized and it is reinforced by that special presence in Christ

In the twentieth century, Karl Barth was the spokesman for a strong movement in Protestant theology which asserted that God's revelation in Christ was related to so-called natural revelation in an absolutely negative way. The rationale for this position is as follows.

It is true that God is present universally in nature, and it is true that man ought to be able to behold this divine presence. The hard truth, however, is that man is a sinner. In saying here that man is sinful, we mean at least this: that he will see things the way he wants to see them, and not necessarily as they are. We all do this. If you want your dinner to taste bad (let's say you had a bad day), it will taste bad, even if it's steak and lobster. If you want the world to be ugly one day, it will be ugly. Of course, it's *your* disposition which makes it that way, but that doesn't seem to matter. This same process occurs when man searches for God. He really doesn't want to find God—for God makes man humble and requires of him certain acts and attitudes which he would rather not be required to do and have. So we search, true, but what we find is what we *want* to find, not the God who is there. As the reformer John Calvin put it, "Man's mind is a perpetual factory of idols." Nazi Germans, for example, searched for and found a god who protects the Fatherland. Racist Americans came up with a god who is supposed to have put a curse on all black people. Sinful man sees what he wants to see.

According to this view, then, man's sin leads him to a false image of God—a god who is worshipped religiously. Religion which is so founded on a perverted natural revelation is thus the epitome of human sin. The religious person, who has created God after his own image, is the most demonic of all. Linguistically, the situation appears totally ironic. We usually think of "religious" as the opposite of "sinful." But we can see, nonetheless, that religion based on a perverted perception of God's natural revelation can be quite demonic.

What then is required if man is to have a right and proper understanding of God? The answer quite simply is a special act of revelation, such as the event of Jesus Christ. Such revelation attacks, negates, and destroys man's natural religion. The unique act of God's revelation counters the human tendency to think of God however man will because in special revelation there is no possibility of misunderstanding what God is like. There is at

Dartmouth College a mural by Orozco which illustrates this negation perfectly. In bright orange and yellow stands Jesus Christ, ax in hand, having just destroyed not only the artifacts of other religions, but also having just chopped down his own cross. The special revelation of God absolutely negates man's natural and religious tendency to "have" a god, be that man pagan, Christian, or whatever. Even so-called Christians, who create God in their own image are felled by the ax.

There is, perhaps, a criterion by which one might distinguish false religion from true religion. If this latter way of relating God's twofold revelation is accurate, it seems clear that false religion is a very comforting sort of thing. God likes you, he agrees with you, he helps you. He is on your side. Such a God does not create trouble for you, asking you to do things you'd rather not do. How could he? After all, you made him up to be the way you wanted him.

The same is not true when faith is a result of God breaking into man's life in an uncompromising way. We might assume that man's first reaction to such an act of God might be, "Oh no! Not me. I like it where I am." We can imagine Abraham's response to God's invitation to move to a promised land. If, for purposes of illustration, we assume the story to be factual, we can almost hear Abraham saying, "You must be kidding, God! I've got all this land, these herds, and plenty of women! Why would I move?" The same was true for Moses: God commanded Moses to lead the Hebrews out of the land and hand of Pharaoh—an idea which did not exactly enchant the intended revolutionary. "But the Israelites won't believe You sent me. They will want signs or miracles." So God gave Moses a magic staff. "But I can't speak well. I won't be able to convince Pharaoh to let the people go. Send Aaron. He knows how to talk." So Moses protested. God's special revelation was a command to leave a safe and secure position, and follow a path of uncertainty and trouble. Then there is Jeremiah. The Israelites were corrupt and the Lord wanted and even forced Jeremiah to protest the injustice and corruption. Jeremiah was a most unwilling prophet, claiming that God deceived him into becoming a critic of the people until he cursed the day he was born. Elijah, another great prophet, was in a cave hiding from Queen Jezebel, who was out for Elijah's skin. There, protected and hidden, Elijah was confronted by God: "Get out of this cave. Go back to the city, to the people, and incite the people to revolution, anointing a new king. Your days of false security are over." In our own day, we can think of Martin Luther King, Jr. Did his faith offer him a life of security and ease—a "religious" life, in the worst sense of the word?

What we see, then, is that when God comes to man something happens which completely negates the comfort and security of man's natural religion. Special revelation creates trouble. This is not to deny that true faith in God also creates in the person a sense of deep joy and responsibility, accompanied by a new feeling of security—a security grounded not in a false piety but rather in God himself. But there is a vast difference between the security offered by an idol who feeds our ego and the security offered by the God who calls man away from his Linus-blanket and thrusts him into the world of racism, starvation, and war.

If we develop this second theme a bit further, it seems natural to ask next: Where and how does God encounter man in such ways that man is torn out of his natural and sinful religion and thrust into a life of responsibility? In other words, if special revelation does negate natural revelation, where and how does God encounter persons in a particular way?

In general, the answer could be: anywhere and anyhow. God could use any means at his disposal to reveal himself to man. For example, beholding a beautiful sunset could create a feeling of humility and responsibility in a person, driving that person away from the idol he has created. However, experiences with nature seem to reinforce natural religion rather than challenge it. Practically all Christians would hold that God comforts man through his word as found in the Bible, which is the account of God's special relationship with Israel and the early church, an account which can also become revelation for men today. The total impact of the biblical message is to tear man out of his self-security, calling him to sacrifice himself for his neighbor, including his enemy.

Besides nature and the Bible, however, it seems that God meets man another way—through fellow human beings. Allow me to illustrate with a personal experience. While in New York attending Union Seminary, my wife and I went downtown for an evening out. All dressed and ready for an evening of fun, we changed at 42nd St. from the downtown Broadway local to the express subway. To switch trains, one has to pass through a tunnel, rather dark and gloomy. As we walked along, we saw in this tunnel an old lady—lying down, dirty with sores, rags for clothes, reaching out a hand and mumbling to passersby. If Jesus ever made the scene in New York, there he was, calling to men through the form and voice of this old lady. Although it is really irrelevant, we walked by as did everyone else. The point is that here, concretely, inescapably, was a fellow human being who was begging and therefore challenging people to stop and help. Now to stop and help would have forced the passersby to leave their own, safe little world, to disrupt their lives, to take a risk. That movement—away from self-interest toward loving responsibility—is what revelation is all about. If we want to generalize, we could say that God encounters us in a special way everytime our fellowman calls upon us for help.

It need not even be so much a call for help; it is the neighbor's breaking into my world which is significant. Sometimes we are just plain lazy and apathetic and the call for help comes to us, inescapable and uncompromising. Sometimes, perhaps you're really down and depressed—and a child comes up before you and smiles. Your private world has been invaded. That, too, can be an act of God's gracious making-himself-known. How often it seems that when everything is going wrong, a fellow human being crosses our path and whispers a "Hey! I love you." And there, at least for the moment, life begins anew. Too often we have separated human from divine love, as if they were totally different. It just may be that God comes to us through the love of other persons. People, it seems to us, moreso than nature and even Scripture, are the how and where of God's revelation.

5

WHAT IS GOD LIKE?

Printed on the currency of the United States is the motto "In God We Trust", just as inserted into the Pledge of Allegiance is the phrase "one nation under God". It's amazing how freely Congress uses a word which is the subject of endless debate and confusion—the word "God"! Suppose you had just read "In God We Trust" to a foreigner, and he asked, "Who is this God in whom you trust?" How would you answer? We commonly assume that everybody knows what God is like, that the word is quite universal. But try it sometime. Ask three different people how they picture God and you will get three different answers. Made aware of this situation, someone will say that every person has the right to his own opinion about God. This sounds very tolerant and democratic, but not exactly enlightened. If, as Christians believe, there is but one God, then it may be that one picture of God is correct while the others are incorrect. Whether man can ever arrive at a correct God-concept, however, is another matter.

If, just for fun, you were to conduct a survey which inquired into the picture or concept which people held of God, you would probably discover that most answers fall into two categories. Generally speaking, God is envisaged either in terms of man or of nature. Beginning with the former, let's take a look at some specific ideas, defining their substance, seeking their origins, and indicating their deficiencies.

Probably the most widely held God-concept is anthropomorphic: God is pictured as the good man with the beard in the sky. He looks like a human being, although he is infinitely wiser, more loving, and more powerful. He lives in some place called heaven, the exact location of which is, as yet, a still undetermined mystery. Our initial impulse is to laugh at this man-in-the-sky theory, which we consider childlike and which we find scientifically unacceptable. And yet, when people pray or even just think about God, subconsciously this anthropomorphic model is in the back of many minds. We find it difficult to conceive of a loving, intelligent being who is not like a man.

The belief is strongly rooted both in tradition and in experience. The Bible is full of anthropomorphic references to God: he speaks, he thinks, he whistles, he loves, he cares, he has a heavenly court, and so on. To this we can add our own personal experience. Anyone who has attempted to answer a child's questions about God knows that anthropomorphic imagery comes the easiest. "God is your Father in heaven. He sees you; he loves you. He is big—very big. And he's older than a million." Anyone raised in western Christianity grows up thinking of God anthropomorphically.

Whereas this style of thinking may be emotionally satisfying, it is not intellectually complete. The first Russian cosmonaut was reported to have announced rather matter-of-factly as he circled the earth, "I find no God up here." The implication, of course, is that God does not exist, as Communists have been saying all along. Some of us might smilingly say that the cosmonaut's conclusion was misguided. Of course God can't be "found" like that, because God is . . . what? . . . further out? Modern cosmology and space travel signify, in principle, the demise of heaven. Heaven, as a place somewhere in the universe where God lives, is no longer a tenable hypothesis. Someone may argue that God is beyond the bounds of the universe, but this argument seems little more than cerebral gymnastics.

The primary value of the anthropomorphic vision is that God's love and personality are maintained to the fullest. But it is a problem as well. If God is *a* being in space, where is he? Any attempt to define or conceive such a location appears ludicrous.

A common variation of this view is a sort of spiritualistic pantheism. Here God is seen as somehow being inside every human being. God is loving, thinking, and present somehow within that mythical human heart. Everyone bears within himself the "spark" of the divine; God lives "in you." The origin of this belief is also traditional and experiential. Passages in the Bible speak of man's body as the temple of God. There has also been an abundance of philosophies which saw man as somewhat divine. But the greatest source for this belief is the personal feeling that God has come to the individual and filled his heart with His divine being.

There is a problem, though, with this sort of spiritualism. Presumably, if all men were killed, God would also die, for God could not exist apart from his human habitation. Or, suppose he could exist disembodied. Is God then a spirit or ghost who travels around the universe? Perhaps, then, with the proper extrasensory perception the Russian cosmonaut might have introduced himself to God.

The last refuge of the anthropomorphic view would be a sort of intelligent, universal World-Spirit. God is spirit, God is intelligent, God is everywhere. Having said that, we can immediately see how far this concept is from the old-man-in-the-sky with which we began. The only element the two have in common, really, is the abstraction of the intelligence, love, and personality of God. But does it make any sense to speak of a World-Spirit who is wise, loving, just? We have in mind, remember, a spiritual reality which is equally omnipresent throughout the universe. It seems questionable whether this concept is tenable, for the attributes of love, wisdom, mercy seem to presuppose a center of being which loves, such as a "mind", a "heart". If one says, "Yes, the World-Spirit has such a center," then we are thrown back to our original question: Where is it?

The second type of God-picture begins with the presupposition that God is a dimension of all reality. He is not *a* being who *is* somewhere. Rather he is present in some way in all reality as part of that reality itself. Paul Tillich, brilliant twentieth-century theologian, argued that God is the "Ground of Being". He is the power which enables being to be, and might be called "Being-Itself". This is not a simple pantheism. Pantheists believe that everything is divine—this book, your pen, trees, and rocks. In pantheism, being is divine. The power of being is different from simple being: it transcends being. Of course, one cannot point to God as the Ground of Being and say, "There he is!" That's the whole point. God does not live in a heaven; he is present everywhere as the power to be.

There is another view which sees reality in terms of *process* rather than just being. The universe is in process, and this process is even more fundamental and primary than that which is in process. In this view, God, therefore, is the "Process-Itself." Most people, however, think neither in terms of being nor of process; they think in terms of energy. Energy is the way many people explain the being of God. Energy is accepted as the common denominator of the universe. It is omnipresent and omnipotent—or at least as potent as anything can be. It doesn't require too great a stretch of the imagination to identify energy with divine being.

The problem with these models of the second type is different from the problem inherent in the anthropomorphic model. There is no need here to ask where God is, for he is everywhere. The great strength of the anthropomorphic model is the fact that it pictures God as loving, personal, caring. It may be asked whether these attributes apply to the God of being, of process, of energy. Does it make any sense? How does Process-Itself forgive man? How does the Ground of Being call Moses to deliver his people from Pharaoh? Protagonists for this latter position, such as Tillich, argue strenuously that the personalism of the anthropomorphic model can be incorporated into the nature model. Without denying absolutely the possibility of this marriage, the great difficulty is obvious. To speak of the Ground of Being as a personal and loving God seems to be stretching words beyond proper usage.

What, then, are we left with? There seems to be an irreconcilable conflict between the two concepts. Either God is pictured as personal, in which case we run into the absurdity of trying to describe where he is, or else God is pictured as the omnipresent basis of reality, in which case we find it difficult to think of him as our personal God. The human mind appears to be frustrated in its attempt to conceive a God.

Therein, however, may lie the problem. If God is indeed transcendent to reality as we know it, it should not surprise us to discover our inability to think of him coherently. Perhaps instead of racking our brains looking for God, we should begin with what God has made known about himself. That is, perhaps our picture of God should be informed by God's own revelation of who he is. Theology, therefore, should begin with revelation. This is the basic Christian approach to the problem. But, as indicated in our discussion of revelation, there is even on this basis no guarantee for agreement. Even basing their thoughts on revelation Christians move in different directions. Remembering the distinction between the negative and the positive ways relating natural and special revelation, let's see how the two ways arrive at a picture of God.

As indicated earlier, some theologians believe that much can be known about God through natural revelation. It is felt that nature about us gives indications of what God is like. He is everywhere, he is all-powerful, all-knowing, all-good. This is a common and certainly respectable notion of who and what God is.

The so-called proofs for the existence of God, which most feel are no proof at all, assert not only that God exists, but also try to show what kind of God he is. Take, for example, the argument from design: There is order and design in the universe. Just as the watch indicates the watchmaker, so the design of the universe indicates a designer, God. The attempt is to show by natural means that God is orderly, intelligent, and artistic. It is, therefore, believed by many that man can naturally know much about God. Of course, there are certain items which we recognize as irrational, requiring special revelation. Such items in particular are the Incarnation and the Trinity. These are dimensions of God's being which are "unnatural" and "irrational" and, therefore, cannot be known apart from special revelation.

On the other hand, there are those Protestant theologians who deny the validity of natural revelation. Here it is felt that God can be known only in the event of Jesus Christ, the unique event of God's self-revelation. Suppose we follow this approach. Suppose we agree that God can be known only in the Christ-event. What, then, can be said of God? Since he sent Jesus Christ, we can say in the first place that God is a God who cares. He loves man and is concerned for human welfare. He is willful in that he has a purpose for mankind. History is headed somewhere. This God is personal, as Jesus was personal. From Christ we get the picture of a loving, caring God, who willingly chose to suffer for the sake of his creatures, a God who intends for man a life of joy and fulfillment. So much is basic. Whether or not Christ tells us more about God is subject to debate, and theologians do debate. For example, some argue that Jesus was nonviolent, therefore God wants us all to follow suit. Others argue that this is not the case, and the debate goes on.

However one proposes to base his discussion of God, he runs into problems. Anthropomorphism seems childlike. Philosophical theism seems cold. The proofs of natural theology are sterile, and the christological approach is at least controversial. It seems to this author, though, that despite the difficulties, the only sane way to arrive at a picture of who God is, is to begin with his self-revelation in the Christ-event.

As a matter of fact, this was how the doctrine of the Trinity arose. The early church knew of a Creator-God, to whom Jesus prayed as "Father". They also knew that after Jesus was crucified and had left them, they experienced another form of divine presence, which they labelled "The Spirit". In other words, the church believed that God had revealed himself in a threefold manner—Father, Son, Spirit—yet without destroying his unity. It was only somewhat later that man's mind began to speculate as to *how* a Trinity was possible. The original doctrine was not based on philosophical ingenuity, but arose out of the church's critical reflection on the divine revelation. To the human mind the Triune God seems infinitely more absurd than a God of Energy. But when the matter is set in proper perspective, it is seen that the God of Energy is no more acceptable to reason than God in Christ, and that if the latter is accepted, the road to full Trinitarianism is wide open.

6

WHAT DOES CREATION MEAN?

The first thought that usually comes to mind when one thinks of Creation is the first two chapters of Genesis. It is a common assumption that the Christian religion teaches that God created the world in six days, resting on the seventh. Beginning with nothing, something new is added each day until, finally, the universe is complete. No doubt there are many Christians who do in fact think that this story, as told in the first two chapters of Genesis, is literally true. They believe that the Bible is the inerrant word of God, containing no error whatsoever. On this basis it is inevitable that a conflict with science should arise. To the biblicist all naturalistic explanations on the origin and growth of the universe contradict the Bible and therefore are wrong. If God created the world in six days, our solar system could not have originated with an exploding star. In some states, where biblical fundamentalism is prevalent, a public school teacher thinks twice before mentioning evolution in the classroom. Although the Monkey Trial is long past, the supposed conflict between Genesis and evolution is still an explosive issue.

Most theologians agree, however, that there is no conflict between science and religion at this point simply because the Bible in no way attempts to explain *how* the world came to be. In order to understand this point of view, consider the first chapter of Genesis itself. Scholarship has shown that this story was compiled by Israelite priests while the whole nation was in captivity in Babylonia, about 450 B.C. It is quite possible that the narrative originated much earlier. But when this chapter was put in the form that we now have, Israel was in a state of bondage. Having once enjoyed independence, the Israelites now found themselves totally destroyed as a nation. Although we cannot know exactly what motivated these exiles either to appropriate or to originate the story of creation, we can hypothesize. By the waters of Babylon they could only question their fate.

Had God deserted them? Was the Babylonian god greater than theirs? Was God in charge here in Babylon, too, or was his jurisdiction limited to Palestine? We can well imagine that the Israelites were shaken by such thoughts. Yet, out of their agony arose a new confirmation of their faith: No, God has not deserted us. He alone is God, in Babylon as in Palestine. These thoughts are set forth in the poetry of "In the beginning God created the heavens and the earth." God, our God, he alone is creator of all. He will deliver us; he will save his people, for all things are in his hands.

It should be clear by now that Genesis 1 is probably not at all an explanation of the origin of the universe. There is absolutely no attempt to explain how the world came to be. This chapter is, rather, an expression of faith, trust, and confidence in God. The account of the seven days is the medium used to express this faith. The message is not the seven days; it is the faith that God is God of all, a God who can be trusted because all times and places are in his hands.

For nonliteralists this means that *any* scientific theory about the origin of the universe is perfectly compatible with the biblical account. Genesis speaks of faith in God; evolution describes a cosmogenetic process. How could there be conflict? Christians have every right and responsibility to judge scientific theories on their own merit, with no question as to whether their faith permits it. The criterion for scientific hypotheses is natural evidence, not religious faith.

At this point, however, a word of caution is necessary. The proper function of science is to explore and understand the evidence given. Unfortunately, some scientists (usually the

poorest) often go beyond the facts and begin to make pronouncements about matters which lie outside the realm of science. In
connection with creation two such pronouncements are: There is
no God, and There is no guidance which is steering the world in a
certain direction. It is at this point that Christian theology, biblicist or not, must take issue with scientism. For no matter what
the extent of one's acceptance of evolution, Christian faith does
assert that there is a God who created. Just what or how he
created is another question. But the fact that there is something
rather than nothing is due to an act of God. This is a statement of
faith. And when a scientist proposes that there is no God, he also
is making a statement of faith—negative to be sure, but nevertheless a statement of faith, for he has no evidence on the matter.
The same holds true with respect to a guiding hand in the course
of evolution. The Christian faith asserts that God created and is
now guiding his creation towards a goal of fulfillment. This is a
statement of faith. When a scientist proposes that there is no such
guidance, he is making a statement not based on evidence, i.e., he
is making a statement of faith. But that is not his job!

Even though a Christian may, therefore, accept evolution, this
acceptance is qualified by two pertinent statements of
faith: First, that there is something is due to God's act. Second,
that despite the helter-skelter character of the evolutionary
process, God is still in control of the situation.

Like Genesis, the doctrine of creation is an expression of faith
and trust. To say that God is Creator is to say that my life and all
that is are in his hands, and he is trustworthy. Not that I ought
therefore to be lazy and apathetic, leaving everything for God to
take care of, but rather that, because God is Creator I am assured
that my life and work are part of a larger order. The doctrine is a
statement of God's relationship to me and to the world, *not* a
theory as to how this world all came to be. Belief in the Creator is
not philosophical speculation. It is always fun to ask such questions as: What was it like before creation? Did God create everything at once? Did he create time? How did he do it? Intriguing

yes, answerable, no. Christian theology is unqualified to answer such questions and denies that it should answer such questions. Again, faith in the Creator expresses a relationship of trust and dependence; it is not the answer to playful speculation. This attitude of trust is expressed in the feeling of being at home in the universe. Faith in the Creator means that one finds oneself in a friendly and hopeful world. There may be total confusion about how the world began, there may be confusion as to what will happen to one next week or next year, but faith in a Creator tempers such confusion and anxiety with the knowledge that ultimately all is well because God is in control, and God loves.

The Christian faith in creation is different from other faiths. Three beliefs offering interesting contrasts to the Christian doctrine are pantheism, deism, and dualism. Pantheism as we saw earlier, is the idea that everything is divine. The whole universe is viewed as a manifestation of divine being—God and matter are one and the same, so that if there were no universe, there would by definition be no God. In contrast, the Christian understanding is that God transcends the world, i.e., is of a different order of being. God is not identical with the matter of space, but—while related to it—is "other than". This otherness of God is usually described in spatial terms: God is "up there in heaven," a certain distance separating him from his creation. We have discussed the difficulty of this view in our chapter on God. We also saw how Tillich seeks to describe the "otherness" of God in terms of a "Ground of Being." However it is described, it is this "otherness" of God which distinguishes Christianity from pantheism, and which is safeguarded by the doctrine of creation.

The second idea to be distinguished from Christianity is deism. Up to and including the Middle Ages, God was believed to be actively involved in the operation of the universe. He held the moon in place, he pushed stars through the sky—in short, the physical operation of the cosmos was dependent upon the constant activity of God. With the advent of modern science the situation changed. Newton's mathematics indicated a world which ran according to certain basic laws, quite independently of divine intervention. The heavenly bodies moved according to the laws of motion and gravity, and not because they were pushed or pulled. The universe became self-sufficient, God unemployed.

But not quite. Although it was true that matters ran quite well without God, certainly someone must have set the whole thing in motion. And so it was recognized that although God may now be sleeping in a closet out in space, He was the One who created it all in the beginning. He created matter and also the laws which govern matter. The picture of the universe which emerged with the rise of science was that of a Machine—the Newtonian World-Machine. The view of God which was part and parcel of Newton's world is called deism. Deism is the view that God created everything in the beginning and set it in motion; but that since then the world is self-sufficient, although God may intervene occasionally, should he choose.

The basic difference between deism and Christian theism is the doctrine of providence. Christians do not believe that God today is in a cosmic convalescent home, recuperating from a one-time act of extreme exertion. God, for Christians, is actively and fully involved in the affairs of the world today. God does not abandon the world he has created. Instead, he deals with it in a loving manner, seeking constantly to guide man on his road to fulfillment. The difference between deism and Christianity centers on the activity of God in the world today.

Finally, there is dualism. Dualism is a powerfully suggestive philosophy which has always run through the minds of men. Basically, it is the idea that there is war in the universe. There is a cosmic struggle between God and Satan. The forces are equal; neither is greater. The fight is on, and the battleground is the heart of man. The battle between the forces of evil and the forces of good are between body and spirit, between dark and light. More often than not, dualism depreciates the body as being evil, the realm of sin and corruption. To escape this body, to fly off to the realm of heavenly spirit—this is seen as salvation.

Dualism was a potent force in the early church. Many of the early Christians were dualists, and it was only after centuries of debate that dualism was finally rejected by the church fathers. It was rejected chiefly because it posited two coequal, coeternal forces. Biblical faith, as we saw in connection with Genesis 1, asserts that God and God alone is in control of the world. He alone is eternal and omnipotent; he alone is trustworthy. Acceptance of a full-fledged dualism by the early church would have been a break with Hebrew thought, a break which early Christians refused to make.

While rejecting an absolute form of dualism, a modified position has been accepted by many Christians through the ages, including today. Saint Paul speaks of the principalities and powers with which we must contend in this world. Other parts of the New Testament speak of the devil and of demons which inhabit living bodies. Supposed witches have been burned at the stake. After a lull, due to the rationality demanded by modern science, dualism is again exerting its force in our society today. The presence of a nether world, inhabited by good angels and evil, is accepted as fact by many people today. Exorcists abound; prayer is said to cast demons out of unwilling bodies. Perhaps the most frightening phenomenon is Satan worship. At least one student in every college class has probably been to a black mass, either as willing participant or frightened observer. Worship of Satan and the glorification of evil have been the cause of more than one death in recent years. Anyone who has seen or read *Rosemary's Baby* and has felt the chill and terror of witchcraft should know that such horror can be found in real life as well.

Beyond doubt, there is today a resurgence of dualistic thought in our time. The cosmic struggle between Good and Evil is felt to be very real, some taking the side of God, others that of Satan. Christians caught up in this phenomenon are not absolute in their dualism. Most believe that although the devil is real, God alone has ultimate power. Such a modified position is certainly compatible with and representative of the doctrine of creation.

Do Christians, then, believe in spiritual beings which are lower than God but higher than man? Depending on who you talk to, the answer may go either way. Angels, devils, and exorcism are real in the minds of many people today, just as they were real in the minds of prescientific man. It is believed, however, that faith and prayer will cast out evil spirits, the implication being, of course, that God is the superior force.

On the other hand, many contemporary Christians belittle belief in demons as being a leftover from a primitive way of thinking. For these people psychological disorder replaces demonic possession. Doctors replace prayer. Racism and war become the enemy, not Satan. In this view man is alone in this world—no ghosts, no devils, no supernatural to fear or contend with. This rejection of any sort of dualism is grounded not only in the scientific frame of mind. To be sure, science has provided natural explanations for events once thought to be the sport of supernatural beings. Even beyond this, though, limited dualism is felt to be contrary to the idea of creation. It can be argued that the doctrine of Creation implies that God and God alone is the supernatural being with whom we have to contend. As created, the world is not "alive." There are no longer "Ghoulies and ghosties and long-leggity beasties, and things that go bump in the night." In this view, events surrounding the birth of Rosemary's Baby are declared null and void by the concept of creation.

The question is open. The basic issue, however, is not whether one believes in demons or not. The issue is whether one believes the Lord to be supreme or not. In other words, Christian theology finds modified dualism acceptable; absolute dualism it rejects.

Whether one believes in the devil or not, one cannot deny that there is evil in the world. But before we proceed, clarification is in order. The so-called problem of evil consists really of two problems, and it is necessary to distinguish between them. There is, first—and we shall consider this later—the problem of human, moral evil. Man is corrupt, selfish, spiteful. The analysis of man represents one problem. The second, which is tied in with creation, is the problem of natural disaster. Earthquakes, floods, cancer, tornadoes—Why? Nature at times seems bent on destruction, and man is forced to ask, Why? The question is not merely academic. Anyone who has had the misfortune to witness bloated corpses left behind by a typhoon or has known one who died of an incurable disease—such a person can only ask in anger, confusion, and heartache: Why? The question has been especially agonizing for Christians who believe that God is omnipotent and good. The problem posed is thus: If God is omnipotent, then—in the face of natural evil—he is not good. But if he *is* good, then he must not be omnipotent. In either case, he is not God. For if God is all-good and all-powerful, why does he allow suffering? That's the question.

Of course, there have been various answers. First it has been argued that suffering is punishment from God. But what if the person involved is innocent? Then, it is said, he must be paying for the sins of his ancestors. This explanation, however, seems hardly compatible with God's love and forgiveness as revealed in Christ. Feeling this, others have argued that suffering is a testing. God is trying to find out how strong a person's faith is, with the accompanying idea that adversity builds character and strengthens faith. It is, however, difficult to the mind and abhorrent to the heart to think of God as testing man through the slaughter of a typhoon or the untimely death of a loved one. Besides, those who propose the testing theory usually also believe in God's omnipotence. If God can do all and *know* all, then surely he knows how the test will work out—so why bother?

Another explanation is needed. Perhaps, it is suggested, perhaps disaster is the work of the devil, not of God. But if this is the case, we must ask why God permits the devil to operate in this way. To test? To punish? And if God cannot overpower the force of evil, perhaps we ought to worship Satan. It is commonly believed that a combination of these forces was operative in the case of Job. A supposedly upright man, Job is thought to have suffered at the hand of Satan because God had wagered with Satan that Job would not falter in his faith. Anyone who would appeal to the case of Job for the answer to the problem of evil should read Job, using a commentary. Job's answer to innocent suffering is no answer at all. God appears in the whirlwind and says, in effect, that his ways are not man's ways. This, to the poet who wrote Job, is the way it is.

But is this the limit to what we can say? What follows is offered as a tentative solution. If it is true that God has revealed himself in Jesus Christ, then that is where we should look for clues as to the meaning of evil. The most obvious fact connected with the Incarnation of Christ is that it was by no means the easiest path God could have chosen to save man. It would have been much simpler for God to snap his fingers and make things to be the way he wanted them. In other words, omnipotent as he was, God yet chose *not* simply to exercise his power. He chose instead to take the path of suffering and agony, culminating in death on a cross. We will argue later that God chose this path because he desired that man should *freely* accept fellowship with God. God did not want to *force* man to do his will. If this is the way God deals with man, it is not illogical to assume that this is also the way that God deals with the world in which man lives. In other words, when God created he freely chose in his omnipotence to *limit* his omnipotence. He willed *not* to exercise freely and forcefully his power whenever he wanted. This means that God does not manifest raw power in the world today. His omnipotence is limited. God created the world in a certain way with certain laws and decided himself to abide by the terms of creation. He created the elements and energy which would form water. Sometimes the water fruitfully waters the crops. At other times it takes life in floods. Neither, specifically, is God's doing. God created the elements and energy which became living cells. Sometimes these cells multiply in normal growth. Other times, uncontrolled division results in cancer. Neither, directly, is God's doing. Just as human beings cry when disaster occurs, so too, does God cry. When creation goes awry, God's heart aches, just as it ached when his Son was nailed to the cross. God's way with the world and with man is to achieve victory without the exercise of his omnipotence. So much is made known in the Incarnation. If we can look at things this way, then there is no problem of evil. Suffering is due neither to Satan nor to a God who tests or punishes. It is, rather, a consequence of God's decision to create and to abide by the terms of his creation. We can find consolation in the fact that God too suffers when his creatures suffer. Greater consolation is found in knowing that God, who created in love and wisdom, has not deserted us, but is still at work in the world to bring his creation to fulfillment.

7

IS GOD STILL ALIVE AND WELL?

It is comparatively easy to believe that there is a God who created the universe once upon a time. It is much more difficult to believe that God is alive and well, and active in the world today. This divine activity in the world today, in which God daily is involved in the affairs of men and nature, is called "providence." In a sense, one could argue that divine providence is at the heart of the Christian gospel, for if God is not today working in the world to accomplish his purposes, then why bother with him? Unfortunately, providence is often confused with other ideas, ideas alien to Christian theology.

One such idea common today is fatalism. Fatalism is the feeling that events in one's life have been determined—quite independently of the will and action of the person involved. Although they really won't admit it, most people who believe in astrology are somewhat fatalistic. How many people do you know who read their horoscopes? Yourself included? Practically everyone knows the "sign" under which they were born. The meaning of all this mystery is the assumption that life has been predetermined for us by the stars and the planets.

Providence is not to be confused with astrological fatalism. The times are in God's hands, not the stars'. Further, as we shall see, man is created free by God, free to exercise his will, to determine his own future. Not only does fatalism encroach on divine providence, it also destroys human freedom.

Besides fatalism there is deism, another idea which contradicts a full view of providence. We saw earlier how deism asserts a one-time creative act, after which God is no longer active in the world. Of course, he may perform a little miracle once in a while, he may occasionally intervene in the affairs of men, but beyond that God is content to amuse himself by himself. In contrast the Christian faith believes that God is working now to shape and guide the history of man towards a goal. According to Christian thought Jesus didn't hang on the cross for the hell of it. Rather, this act is a sign that the God who was present in Christ is present also today.

Deism is rejected; so also is fatalism. In their place, Christian faith asserts a rather wonderful sort of relationship between God and man. God creates man free and calls upon man to work with God to create a better world. God and man cooperate to overcome the evils and injustices prevalent among men. God cares about the wretched and damned of the earth, and calls upon men to work freely with him. This, at least, is one picture as to what God's up to when we say he is "working in the world today." There are other models of providence, and we shall consider them below. First, however, there is a question which must be looked into. In whatever way one wishes to describe *what* God is doing, he must answer the question *how*? How is God doing whatever he is doing?

Most theologians would probably agree that whatever God does in the world, he does through natural means. That is, he does not present himself openly as one force among other forces. God may save the life of a person "through" the hand of the surgeon. He may establish justice "through" a law passed by Congress. He may elect a pope "through" the politicking of Rome's cardinals. How is God doing these things? He does them "through" purely natural means. But, suppose we ask how God saves a person through the skill of the doctor? How does he affect the doctor? By influencing the doctor to concentrate? How? By . . . . It is easy to assert that God works in the world through natural means. It is less than easy to describe just how this involvement takes place. It is at this point where the theologian can justifiably say, "This is where reason runs out. It's a mystery."

Another option would be to maintain a direct divine involvement. God is said to act blatantly as a force among forces, so that one could say that God did this, and nobody else. Such acts are called miracles. A miracle could be defined as an act of God which is *not* mediated through natural means but which is directly attributable to God. Whether or not God acts in such a way is the subject of endless debate. There are people who believe without doubt in miracles, there are total sceptics, and there are people who hold a variety of positions somewhere in between. The spectrum of opinion is present in the history of thought and the debate rages today between "Jesus Freaks" and persons of more doubting inclination.

Many people reject miracles because miracles contradict scientific fact. A miracle by definition stands outside the realm of natural events and is therefore unacceptable to a mind committed totally to a scientific attitude. But it may be asked whether it is proper to make science the norm as to what God can and cannot do. Modern liberals, in their devotion to science, tend to limit God's power arbitrarily. That is, denial of miracles is predicated on a norm which stands outside the realm of theology, i.e., the scientific norm. Such a procedure is questionable.

In view of this difficulty, many nonliberals rather forcefully assert that God can do anything he wants—whether it contradicts laws of nature or not. So they believe that God, in his omnipotence, performs miracles. Let us suppose, then, that God has done such a deed, that he has cured a person of cancer. A genuine miracle has truly occurred. But why only one? Why doesn't God cure every person? The earth is filled with people sick, starving, impoverished. Why, if God is willing and able to intervene miraculously, does he not do so? What kind of deity is it who can heal but will not? Believers in miracles must answer such questions.

Usually, they say something like: "This person was healed

because his faith was strong. He believed God would cure him, and this belief effected the cure. People who are not healed simply do not have the necessary faith." This answer sounds plausible enough but is really a pitiable evasion. In the first place, Christianity does not believe that faith is something for which man is rewarded. Faith is founded on grace, which is a gift from God. Even so, what of those suffering persons who do not know God? As we hear of massacre in Biafra and in Bangla Desh, what are we to say? That God could miraculously intervene, but would not, because the victims were not pious Christians? It is no wonder that people are atheistic; a God who can heal but refuses is worse than no God at all. A God able to feed starving children, but who does not, deserves the scorn of man, whether he rot in hell or not. In such a case, hell would be an honor. For such reasons, it seems to us that God must be said *not* to perform miracles. Unexplained happenings are to be viewed as events whose cause is not yet known. But we do not deny miracles because science tells us to. Not at all. If we suppose that God has revealed his ways in the event of Jesus, then we ought to look at that event for a clue as to whether God performs miracles or not.

The first thought is that of course Jesus did miracles—and does so today. And apparently Jesus indicated that: "Your faith has made you well." Now some argue that Jesus did heal during his lifetime, but this power is no longer with man; hence no miracles today. But it can also be questioned on theological grounds whether Jesus ever performed a miracle. The central point of the Incarnation is the reconciliation between man and God accomplished uniquely on the road to the cross. The way of the cross is the way of humility and "soul-power." Victory is achieved through suffering—not through open acts of divine power. Jesus was tempted, according to the Gospels, tempted to perform miracles to save his own skin. But he steadfastly refused. Read the stories of temptation in the wilderness and of the tormenting during his last days. The question posed is this: Are miracles compatible with the way of the cross? Are open manifestations of divine power compatible with the "soul-power" that filled the man Jesus? It does not seem inconceivable to us to think that the cross itself is the greatest witness that God does not act openly and directly in this world. If it is rebutted that Jesus was raised from the dead, and that this certainly is new and miraculous, it should be remembered that this has happened to Jesus alone and that, because of his unique relationship to the Father, an absolutely unique relationship, it does not seem inconsistent to affirm this miracle while doubting others.

It is not our intent here to deny miracles. It is our purpose, however, to indicate the profound difficulties encountered if one does in fact believe in such direct divine acts. We have also attempted to show that careful attention to the revelation in Christ may indicate that God's way with the world is not the way of miraculous intervention.

Another topic connected with providence is prayer. What is prayer and does it really affect God? Does it make sense to pray? The questions admit of no easy answer. Prayers of thanksgiving present no problem. To thank God for the blessings of life is a natural expression of faith. It is only the prayers of petition—asking God for something—which are problematic. The Christian gospel asserts that God loves man and that God is actively working for the fulfillment of human life. Whatever man could rightfully and selflessly ask of God, God is already doing. "Give us this day . . . , forgive us our trespasses . . . ." Before and apart from our prayer God is already doing these things. Why, then, must we ask for what is currently happening? In response, some have said prayer is more for the pray-er than it is for God. Prayer is man's expression of trust that God too is concerned about those things for which man prays. As such an expression, prayer has value. But that it causes God to "change his mind" is questionable. A popular understanding is that prayer is really a person talking to himself: a sort of self-psychoanalysis that makes a person feel better. This can be beneficial, but if this is the extent of prayer, then it would be better to talk to someone who can answer back, such as a friend; for talking to oneself seldom provides the encounter and criticism necessary for growth. Whatever prayer is, it is more than conversation with oneself.

Let us return to the earlier question regarding the what-dimension of providence. The writer has already given tentative expression to the idea that God holds a loving and free relationship with man. It is time now to give direct attention to other ideas about what God is doing in the world.

Probably the most widespread idea is the "personal salvation" syndrome. What God is doing in the world is saving persons from their sins. He sends his Holy Spirit, who guides the individual to seek the good and, failing at that, to seek forgiveness. The ultimate goal is seen as heaven. God is preparing a place for those who believe, he is girding up their faith in the meantime. There are corollaries to this syndrome, but the key concept is that providence entails God's working to "save" people from their sins in order that they may go to heaven when they die.

Another description of God's providential activity relates to the establishing of God's kingdom on earth. God here is not just marking souls for heaven; rather he is working for human wholeness this side of death. Where there is injustice, God is striving to overcome it. Where there is hatred, God seeks love. Hunger, poverty, racism, war—all of these and more are contrary to God's will for man. Because God, in this view, works through natural events, he is seen as being involved in and operating through social and political change. God's purpose is the creation and maintenance of the *human* nature of life, and this purpose is achieved through those people who also work for this goal.

A specific illustration of this general view is the thought of James Cone, black American theologian. According to Cone, the message of the gospel is liberation. Jesus went to the poor and outcast of society, offering them inspiration and hope, while at the same time denouncing the oppressors, the rich and the powerful. Liberation, not heaven—that is what the Christian faith is all about. Further, wherever movements of liberation are occurring in the world today, there is where the gospel is being acted out. What is God doing? He is liberating oppressed peoples, leading them into social, political, and economic freedom—not marking them for a heavenly afterlife.

We have asked the how and the what questions; we need now a final word on who. Who is included in the redemptive work of this provident God? On the most abstract level there are three answers: nobody, somebodies, everybody. That God cares for nobody is just plain contrary to Christian faith. The issue boils down, therefore, to: everybody or not? Although we shall deal with the question more fully when we consider the doctrine of man, we can here lay down the various alternatives. Some people feel that God wants to save everybody, but that many reject God's offer. Those who are saved are those who believe. To this it can be countered that faith is itself a gift from God—and that the fact that some people have faith and others do not is evidence that God wants to save some persons and not others. This is the so-called doctrine of double predestination—that God has elected certain people to salvation, others to damnation. The third alternative rejects both positions. Instead, it says, God's love includes every man, whether accepted or not. That is, everybody is saved, however salvation is defined.

All three answers have their deficiencies. Double predestination creates the image of a rather arbitrary and terrifying God, one whom man might quite rightfully reject. The first alternative places the outcome of salvation squarely on man, minimizing the necessity of grace. The third alternative seems to place all the significance on grace, minimizing totally the role of human decision and responsibility. If one had to choose, the only option which seems to contradict the love revealed in Christ is that of double predestination. The least one can and ought say is that God loves every man and seeks to fulfull the life of every man. Every man, in consequence, is called to live in love and responsibility in this God-given life. God damns no man; rather, the context for all human life is divine love.

8

WHAT IS MAN?

There are a number of different perspectives from which to look at man. Biology looks at the ways that cells function in living organisms. Sociology studies the interrelationships between people in society. The psychiatrist seeks out causes and cures for men's mental illnesses. The theologian, in his turn, considers man in his relationship to God. The subject of this chapter is man as a creature of God.

The Judeo-Christian tradition has been by no means modest in its claims about man. Man is seen as the high-point of creation, created in the very image of God himself. He is given charge of the earth, to be God's steward, naming the animals and tilling the soil. In the Hebrew mind, to name something was in part to create it. Hence the statement that Adam named the animals indicates the proximity of Adam's position to that of God Himself. Further, Christians find at the heart of the New Testament the claim that *God* became *man*. What greater argument for the superiority of man than to say that God took on human flesh?

But the claim is not made without difficulty. The absolutely unique position which the Hebrew-Christian tradition attributes to man is problematic. What really, in the final analysis, makes a man different from his dog, so that the man is created "in the image of God" but the dog is not? What is so unique and special about man that the Son of God should become *homo sapiens*, and die in that flesh? Throughout the ages, Christian or not, men have held the view that man was superior to the animals, mostly because man had a "spirit" which his dog lacked. Never clearly defined, this spirit was variously spoken of as reason, or mind, or soul. Modern man has presumed that he had this "something spiritual" which his animal friends lacked.

Anyone who has seen the movie *Planet of the Apes* has to think twice the next time he looks at the monkeys in the zoo, because on that mythical (?) planet, ape is the organism which thinks and speaks, not man. Indeed, according to their scripture, "God created ape in his image"; and two chimpanzees who try to show that ape has evolved from the lower form, man, are quickly repudiated by fundamentalist ape theologians. By what right, we may ask, do *we* make so bold a statement as to claim that *man* is created in the divine image? Has evolution now ceased, and a *post-homo sapiens* species will never arise? The *Planet of the Apes* and the Bigfoot, California cousin to the Abominable Snowman, can be seen as echoes of the biblical question: "Man, what art thou . . .?"

The question of human spirituality can be put in another context. The most unnerving aspect of LSD is not the hallucinogenic effects, but the implication that spirit (reason, mind, soul) can be reduced to a series of electro-chemical interactions. If this is the case, what is it, then, that really makes me so distinct from my dog? Is man *qualitatively* different, having something that animals don't have and in principle never could have? Or is man superior simply because his cerebral network is more highly advanced and refined?

It should be clear that man's exalted view of himself is not something to be accepted lightly. The question of who man is, is a complex question not only for theology but also for science and history as well. A simple but short-sighted solution is to say that man is unique, that he has a God-given spirit which other organisms lack, and that no creature higher than man will ever evolve. People who argue this way usually also take literally the biblical stories of Adam and Eve. That is, they believe that God zapped into existence two persons, and placed them in the Garden. Anyone who cares to discover that this story in Genesis is *not* to be taken literally, need only consult a scholarly commentary. Genesis 1 and 2 are not history as we know it. But just because this particular account is rejected as a historical source, does not mean that the evolution of man from lower forms of life is necessarily true. God may have created *homo sapiens* out of nothing—although such a theory seems very unlikely and is by no means a necessary part of what Christians believe. We do not intend to argue here about the theory of evolution, but only to indicate the difficulties involved in literal interpretation.

There is a related question which can be more easily clarified. It is commonly assumed that according to the Christian religion man is made up of a body and a soul. There is a strong tradition, beginning with the New Testament, which supports this body/soul dualism. Although uncertain as to just when the soul was created, this tradition is agreed that the soul will never die, i.e., it is immortal. Further, in some manner good souls will go to heaven, bad souls to hell.

There is, however, another tradition in Hebrew-Christian thought which is equally weighty. The early Hebrews rejected any notion of man being made up of two distinct parts. Man, for them, was a whole being. He had physical and spiritual dimensions, and these were dimensions of but one being. In the fullest sense of the word, they saw man as a psychosomatic being. As a consequence of this view, most Hebrews did not believe in any sort of afterlife. When the body died, the whole man perished. There was no soul which continued to exist.

It is nevertheless true that much of the early church was dualistic, believing in an immortal soul. It is generally agreed, however, that the idea of the soul did not have its roots in the Hebrew tradition but rather was imported from various other religions and philosophies, Greek and Persian in origin. As indicated, though, there were early Christians who believed with the Hebrews that man was a psychosomatic unity, one being, with physical and spiritual dimensions. With the Hebrews, they also believed that when man died, he died; there was no immortal soul which lived on. But faith in the Resurrection of Jesus from the dead introduced a new element—that man, though dead, would be raised in the future into a new kind of bodily being. Man, created, would be re-created at the resurrection. Thus, the Apostle's Creed speaks of "the resurrection of the body" and the Nicene Creed looks for "the resurrection of the dead." The thought is not that of an immortal soul which inhabits the body and which survives physical death, but rather of a whole man who dies and is later resurrected. It seems that this latter approach is both more biblical and also truer to the reality of man. If this is correct, it would be proper to say that Christian theology does not believe in the existence of immortal souls. Man, as a creature of God, is a whole being.

As such a being, man lives within a certain relationship between himself and God. This relationship is aptly described in Genesis 1 and 2 as one in which man is given charge over the earth, to care for it as God's steward. In his day-by-day living, man is to love and live responsibly with his fellowman, so that together they live in harmony and peace before God. Whoever man is, and however he is related to the apes, this much is clear: he is called by God to be a loving, responsible member of a human community.

Man seems not to have answered that call, however. The history of mankind is not a history of love and peace, but of war and distrust. There is little doubt that men do not live in harmony with each other, that they do not accept responsibility one for another. This state of affairs, according to Christian thought, is a manifestation of what goes by the name of sin. Everyone, theist and atheist, agrees that man is, at least at times, unloving, but not everyone believes man is sinful. The distinction is this: to say that something is sinful is to say it is contrary to God's will. If someone does not believe in God, he does not believe in sin, although he may agree that man is unloving. Statements about sin, therefore, are really statements of faith, not merely empirical judgments about how bad man is.

9

WHAT IS SIN?

There are some clearly defined dimensions of sin which are agreed upon by most theologians. We can begin by saying that sin is not immorality; it may be immoral, but it need not be. Take the following cases. Imagine a woman with a young child in an area recently taken over by an occupation army. Finding absolutely no work, and faced with imminent starvation for herself and her child, she turns to prostitution. Imagine, on the other hand, an upright citizen who continually refuses to hire qualified blacks for work in his office. In terms of social acceptance the prostitute is labelled "immoral" while the "good" citizen is not. But in terms of who is acting lovingly and who not, we could say that the prostitute can make a good case before God and the gentle man cannot. There is an important distinction to be made between sin and social immorality. God judges the one, man the other.

The same is true with respect to crime. Consider another example. A young boy lives in a ghetto. His unskilled mother works all day, bringing home a little money to support him and his sister; his father is dead. Hungry, and knowing that his sister too is undernourished, he steals food continually from the local grocer. Judged by the laws of society he is a criminal; stealing is illegal. But is his activity sinful? If we say that acts motivated by love are commanded by God, then the boy's stealing is criminal but it is not sinful.

Just as sinfulness is not to be seen merely as immorality or as criminality, so too it is not to be viewed merely as *act*. Sin nvolves more than doing a bad thing every once in awhile. rresponsibility and lack of love are somehow grounded in the very nature and attitudes of men. Sin is not only an act of man; it s also grounded in his very being. Our thoughts, our attitudes, our states of mind are the springboard for sinful acts. The acts proceed from a disposition of the heart which is selfishly self-oriented. There is a kind of interdependence between man's acts and his being: the acts are founded upon the inner disposition, and this disposition is reinforced by the acts. Sin is not merely a bad thing we do; it is characteristic of our whole state of being.

A related idea is that sin is not something purely personal but s also a communal phenomenon. Many institutions in our society, for example, have been labelled racist. It is felt that somehow a racist attitude pervades the institution itself. Or, if one considers Nazi Germany, it is easy to see how aggressiveness and hatred develop within the society and the individual simultaneously. Another example closer to many students is the custom of fraternity and sorority "rushing." Would-be brothers or sisters visit the chapterhouse, trying to impress everyone so that they will be accepted into the organization. After the visitors go home to await news of their fate, they become the butt of cruel and humiliating analysis. At the fraternity house all the brothers sit around and talk about the "worth" of the rushees, and if one rushee does not fit their image of what he should be, everyone makes fun of him behind his back. The interesting point s that *individually* the fraternity brothers would probably treat the loser in at least a humane fashion. But *together*—that's another story. In group enterprises, human irresponsibility merges in forms which go beyond what the individual alone is capable of. Sin is not merely the act and state of being of the individual, but of the society as well.

If these are some dimensions of sin, what is sin itself? To this question there have been a variety of answers. Sin has been described as rebellion against God which arises out of human pride. Adam wanted to be like God, so he ate the apple. These twin concepts of pride and rebellion have been most prominent in the history of Christian thought. In recent years, however, another concept of sin has made itself known. The presupposition is that man is created by God to accept responsibility, freely and lovingly, responsibility to live in peace with his neighbor and in harmony with the earth. Failure in this task is seen as the essence of man's sin. Irresponsibility is what sin is all about. Inasmuch as responsible living involves certain tasks, failure to be what we are intended to be could be described as laziness or apathy. Certainly the word "apathy" strikes a familiar note with students today. Irresponsibility, apathy, a refusal to be the *human* being God intends us to be, these are the manifestations of human sin. If, as we indicated in connection with providence, God is working in the world to create conditions of justice, dignity, and equality for all men—if this is what God is doing in the world today, then sin is a refusal on man's part to participate in this divine activity. In his act and in his being, individually and collectively, sinful man refuses to participate in God's desire to make human life human.

The results of this irresponsibility are primarily four, pertaining to God, others, self, the earth. Because he is proud, or apathetic, or both, man has fallen out of his proper relationship with God. Instead of being God's co-worker, sinful man becomes the obstacle to God's saving activity. Secondly, man no longer lives in loving fellowship with other people. We cannot even look someone else in the eye without feelings of uneasiness. There is distrust, jealousy, hatred, and a general inability to live together in mutual aid and assistance. Wars are the obvious example on the big scale, arguments with friends and families on a small scale. Thirdly, man finds it difficult to live with himself. The innocence and wholeness of a flower child is but a dream. Every human being is confronted with the question of the meaning of his life and easy answers are not forthcoming. The suicide is the most obvious case in point—a person who cannot find a positive answer to why he should live. Most people, though, seek less dramatic solutions to the question of life's meaning. Some thrive on success and fame. Others on busy-ness, activity to occupy what would otherwise be unnerving reflection. Many today take drugs. Flight to chemical excitement indicates that life as it is, is not as it ought to be.

Inability to live with God, with others, with ourselves—and finally, sin manifests itself in our inability to take care of the earth. Man was created to take charge of his environment, to live in it and with it in a responsible way. It is becoming painfully clear that man has failed on this score also. So much has been written lately on environmental problems that we need not belabor the point. But there is, it seems, an intrinsic connection between environmental disaster and man's sinful refusal to accept his God-given task of caring for the earth.

It has been argued that death is also a result of man's turning away from God. How often have we heard that "the wages of sin is death"? But it is by no means obvious that God intended man to be immortal in the first place. If man is a creature, why should he not accept death as the ultimate certification of his finitude? In other words, it can be easily argued that man was created mortal, and that, sin or not, man's finite existence would ultimately terminate.

There are three major questions connected with the doctrine of sin which are extremely problematical. They pertain to the universality, totality, and origin of sin. Let us consider universality first. We have already stated that man is created free—free to live responsibly, or not. On the other hand, it is a basic Christian understanding that all men are sinners. The question pertains to the compatibility of these two statements. If man is free, can he not avoid sin? If man is free, how can Christians believe that all men are sinful? In other words, on what basis does Christian theology argue that *all* men are sinful beings?

There have been at least three general theories which seek to explain how or why it is that sin is a universal fact. The first theory may be labelled "the biological transmission theory." Here we find a belief that Adam and Eve were created pure and innocent. Unfortunately, they decided one day to eat the forbidden fruit and, as a consequence, they lost that original purity in which they had been formed. Inasmuch as the whole human race is descended from this original pair, the race inherits from them a sinful flesh. This reasoning explains why today many parents have their baby baptized almost immediately after birth. They are afraid lest the child die before the taint of inherited "original" sin can be erased by baptism. It is difficult, however, to lend credence to this theory. It seems a bit far-fetched to think that somehow, biologically contained in the sperm and the egg, lies the cause of human corruption, although it must certainly be admitted that genetic inheritance plays a large role in the development of character.

A much more reasonable theory is that of "imitation." We all grow up and live in an environment where we learn from the example of others. Parents can affirm this theory as they observe their younger children learning from the older. Competition for toys, deceit in getting mommy's sympathy, crying for attention—all these tricks so common to children can be seen being picked up daily by the growing child. When parents despise people on welfare, so too will the children; when they make derogatory remarks about the color of someone's skin, the children will follow suit. It does indeed seem quite reasonable to argue that sin is learned by observing others.

But what would happen if the following experiment were set up? A group of embryonic human beings are taken from the moment of their conception and isolated from all corrupted society. Somehow they develop and grow with only each other for company, totally ignorant that there are other human beings. What would happen? Any answer, of course, is purely hypothetical. Many people would guess, however, that rivalry, selfishness, greed, and all the rest would develop in quick order. Golding's *Lord of the Flies* certainly points in this direction. In other words, human corruption is not merely a learned phenomenon, but is rather in the condition of man himself—as distinguished from biological sinfulness. (And yet—there may be living evidence to the contrary. There was recently discovered deep in the Philippine jungles a Stone Age tribe known as the Tasaday. Prehistoric, this small tribe would seem to contradict all theory about the innate aggressiveness of mankind. Gentle and affectionate, these people lack in their vocabulary any word for war. There is no division of labor, food is shared, and the awareness of personal property is almost negligible. Peaceful contentment seems to pervade their communal existence. It could be that the Tasaday innocence shows that, given a proper environment, the sinfulness of human beings can be overcome.)

Some theologians, however, have presented arguments which try to show that sin is rooted in the very structure of human existence. One such theory, for example, might center on death. Man is aware he must die, but the prospect frightens him. Fear leads to anxiety, which in turn prevents a proper exercise of love and responsibility. Or, instead of death, one could consider man's ability to imagine. Man can think of himself as he would like to be—rich, dashing, handsome—but isn't! So he tries to be what he is not—and in the process he takes advantage of other persons, building up his ego and wealth by detracting from theirs. Here, as with death, the cause of sin is seen as rooted in the very structure of human life. Sin, therefore, is a universal, inescapable phenomenon.

The weakness of this view is that it seems to make sin a result of man's finitude. That is, it is because man must die that he sins; it is because he is limited that he sins. This result is unacceptable because it is basic to Christian thought that man is created *good* and that there is nothing sinful about being a limited, finite creature of God. This theory, therefore, as the other two, is deficient.

The long and short of the matter is that whereas Christians assert sin to be a universal phenomenon they have *no* theory which satisfactorily explains how or why all men are sinful. There may be some truth in each of the theories, but even collectively they are not adequate. Why are all men sinful? There is no answer. Are all men sinful? As a matter of faith, yes. Perhaps also as a matter of observation!

The second major problem concerns the totality of sin. Is man completely incapable of love? Is he totally irresponsible? Or are there dimensions in man which may be described as good? This is one of the questions on which Catholic and Protestant thought has been somewhat divided, although exact differentiation is difficult. Let's take a concrete example: A man very gently helps a nice, little old lady cross a busy street. For the purpose of illustration, we'll say the man is an atheist. Is this a sinful act, or not? Catholic theology would say first of all that this was certainly an act worthy of civil admiration. That is, judged by the norms of society, it was a good and moral thing to do. But it has further value; it is the kind of thing that God wants man to do. Therefore, helping the lady across the street is at least a step in the right direction—and it is certainly better than knocking her down and stealing her purse. So we find in Catholic thought the ideas of different kinds of sin and differing degrees of sinfulness.

The same is not true in basic Protestant thought. The act would here too be praised as a civil thing to do. In society charity is better than criminality. But Protestant theology generally maintains that only a good tree brings forth good fruit. If a person has not received the power of the Holy Spirit, he can do nothing which is *not* sinful. Sin is sin is sin—and there are no varying degrees of sinfulness. All human acts, apart from grace, are equally condemned in the eyes of God. To be a Boy Scout is no better than to be part of a street gang.

In the Protestant mind, therefore, man is totally a sinner. There is no "part" which escapes corruption. Consequently, whereas certain acts may appear to be civilly applaudable, before God all are equally condemned as the acts of sinful men. The problem with this view is obvious. There *is* a difference between helping somebody and hurting him, and whatever motivations lurk in our subconscious, it must be better—even in God's eyes—

to help rather than hurt. To condemn all things as equally sinful just does not seem very helpful.

Catholic thought escapes this dilemma. It sees the human reason as capable of not sinning and therefore capable of turning toward God and helping one's neighbor. That is, in the Catholic mind, man is *not* totally sinful, but can at least begin to move in the right direction. The possible weakness of this position may be exactly the strength of the Protestant view: does it account for the depth of human corruption? Is reason capable of standing above sin, even to the slightest degree? Man's capacity for self-delusion, for rationalization, and for *not* reasoning, seems endless. Anyone who has ever argued with a full-fledged racist knows that the appeal to reason is fruitless. Having already made up his mind, "reasons" abound why his argument is right.

Is man totally sinful? Problems arise if we say yes; questions arise if we say no. A similar dilemma surfaces if we inquire into the origin of sin, and this is the third major problem. Few would deny the presence of sin in our lives, the lack of love of men for each other. But how did it happen that man came to sin? For simplicity's sake, let us avoid the questions of biological inheritance and imitation. Let us assume that we are considering the first persons who ever were. Created free, they sinned. Why? In answering this question we should take notice of the fact that "before" sin there is temptation, temptation to reject God's will, to be irresponsible toward one's fellowman. If we assume that man of his own free will gives in to temptation, our question becomes: whence temptation? What is there that tempts man so much that he freely and willingly gives in to the temptation?

One answer, of course, is the devil. Not that "the devil made me do it." The notion that man is *forced* to sin is contrary to Christian faith. But that "the devil *tempted* me to do it"—that is certainly a possible explanation. And so we find poor, gullible Eve as the victim of a wise and subtle serpent, the masquerade of the devil. There can be no doubt that Satan as Tempter has had a prominent position in the history of the church.

For those, however, who find it impossible to accept a horned creature with cloven hoof, there is another possibility. Quite apart from positing a devil, it is quite possible to conceive of temptation as given within the structure of existence itself. In this view man is created, not sinful, but tempted. Temptation is part of life itself. However, we must not confuse temptation with the desire to perform immoral acts. Temptation refers to the much broader possibility of refusing to live in love and responsibility. Take the myth of Adam and Eve. There is that apple, hanging on the tree, of which God had commanded: "Thou shalt not eat." Then Eve eats—not because the snake whispered in her ear, but because she had decided—freely—to disobey God. Suddenly, she is found out by Adam. What does Eve do? She blames it on the snake: "He made me do it." Here we can see that Eve's relationship with her animal friends is now broken, and with Adam, too—for she *lied* in blaming it on the serpent. Eve's relationship with others are no longer loving, and so are broken. Again, they are broken not because of the devil, but because the temptation or possibility of unlove is given with the commandment to love. If we are freely to be responsible there is, by definition, the given possibility of being irresponsible.

If we extrapolate from this myth and apply it to ourselves, the following picture emerges. We exist as human beings within a context of interpersonal relationships. The human possibility is to act in a loving and responsible manner. But because this possibility is there, the opposite is also an option: you're at a party somewhere, and one of the persons present is someone you "just can't stand." This person comes over to you and tries to strike up a conversation. In this situation, you can either open yourself up, try to overcome your preconceptions, and act like a human being, or else you can "shut off" that person. To be tempted is to entertain the latter course of behavior, and this possibility is present in all our life-situations. To repeat, if we are freely to be responsible there is, by definition, the given option of being irresponsible.

One implication is that human perfection does not consist in the absence of temptation, but in the absence of sin. What makes human life human is the constant refusal to succumb to temptation. In other words, if this latter view is correct, human life is a struggle—a struggle to be persistent in the responsible use of freedom. Paradise does not consist in the dull routine of white clouds and green fields. It consists in the continuous struggle to live with others in love, refusing in freedom to turn love to our selfish advantage. Jesus, according to the gospels, was tempted; but he did not give in. With this as our example, we can see that to be human means to overcome temptation, not to avoid it. For that is impossible.

10

WHO IS JESUS CHRIST?

There is no doubt that Jesus Christ is the focal point of Christian faith. From his life until ours, Christians of all stripe have held that their faith is bound up with Jesus the Christ. Here, if at all, one could expect simplicity and clarity and yet it is in thinking about Jesus that some of the most perplexing questions arise, and all of the questions are interdependent. In the attempt to facilitate discussion we have divided the material into two questions: Who is Jesus Christ? and What did he do for man? Although the material is divided thus, it really cannot be separated, for what he did was dependent on who he was, and vice-versa.

Who was Jesus Christ? A variety of answers have been given to this question, although only one has been accepted by the church at large. One could say that Jesus was a man, a good man, an intelligent man, but, in the final analysis *only* a man. This view was held by some early Jewish Christians who were strictly monotheist. They felt that to say Jesus was more than a man, to say he was the Son of God, would be polytheism. So they rejected any notion of Christ being divine. Another possibility is to say that Jesus started out as a normal human being, and that he was good and perfect in every way. He was so perfect, in fact, that God chose to adopt Jesus as his Son, to live henceforth with him in eternity. Such a position, not surprisingly, is called "adoptionism ."

These views were unacceptable to the early church for reasons dealing with salvation. To put it most simply, they felt that man was a sinner and that only God could "save" man from his sin. That is, whatever it took to re-create love and responsibility in man was not to be found in man; salvation could come only from God. The man Jesus, no matter how perfect he was, did not qualify as a savior if he was *only* a man. Even if he was later adopted, he is not thereby made equally and fully God. Adoptionism, therefore, is also rejected. Whoever Jesus was, it was felt that he must be fully and truly God, else he could not save mankind.

There was another tendency in the early church which headed in the opposite direction. Beginning with the idea that Jesus Christ was fully divine, some groups concluded that he really could not be a true man. To be sure, Jesus had walked the earth, and people had seen and touched him. But in one way or another these people felt that there was something about Jesus which just was not normal. Some said he really didn't have a physical body; it only looked that way, as some sort of a trick. Some felt that Jesus had a body but that the center of his personality, such as his mind, or spirit, or "heart," was divine. Probably many Christians today share this view. They see Jesus as a man—but one with the mind of God, which, of course, enables him to know all things, to be perfect, to perform miracles.

Such positions, however, were also rejected by the majority of the early church. *Man* was the sinner, and if *man* is to be saved, the *savior* must be *man*. It may not seem obvious to us to require that Jesus be fully man. Why could not God—or God's mind in the form of Jesus—save men? The insistence on the part of the church that Jesus be fully man is understandable only in connection with the theories of *how* Jesus supposedly saved man. Perhaps the next section of this chapter will shed light on this point. Suffice it to say now that while being fully God, Jesus was viewed by the church as also being fully man.

Jesus Christ, fully and completely man, fully and completely God. To this must be added: in one person. It's not as if there were two Christs, perhaps at two stages of time. No, only one Jesus Christ, fully God and fully man in one person. This is orthodox Christian faith in the best sense of the word, for all other options were rejected by Church Councils as heretical. The how of it is an unanswerable question. Any attempt to explain how Jesus Christ is true God and true man must falter on the paradox, and any attempt to say less than "full God, full man" is declared heretical.

It has been held by some that the "virgin birth" theory is an answer to the how question. With Mary for a mother and God for a father, it seems natural to say that he was true God and true man! On the other hand, it could be asked whether the absence of a human father does not jeopardize the true humanity of Jesus. How is it possible to speak of a fully human being when that person lacks the paternal elements in procreation? Suppose, on the other hand, that Joseph in fact was Jesus' father. There is no reason why this, of necessity, should preclude the possibility of his also being "true God." In other words, the virgin birth does not guarantee that Jesus was true God and instead seems to destroy his humanity. On the other hand, had Joseph been his father, this need not destroy his divinity and would certainly preserve his humanity. Should one accept the virgin birth as literally true, one should not thereby use it as an explanation for "true God, true man in one person."

In pursuing this question of who Jesus was, at least three other questions present themselves. Was he sinless? Did he perform miracles? Did he know who he was? There is no doubt that most Christians today would answer each in the affirmative, and yet the questions are sufficiently unique to warrant individual attention. Taking the first question, we can say that it is orthodox doctrine that Jesus was sinless. According to the Council of Nicaea, A.D. 325, Jesus is like us in all things except sin. The problem that naturally comes to mind is this: if Jesus is true man, and if man is sinful, how can Jesus be sinless? Is this not a logical contradiction? The answer depends on one's perspective.

If "true man" is indeed sinful man, then there is contradiction. But it may be that true man means sinless man, man as he was created to be, before he fell into sin. In that case, Jesus alone would be true man, and we would only be poor imitations thereof. Of course, here again sin is not to be identified with cheap immorality. Jesus no doubt became angry at times, but then anger is not always sinful. It can be said, then, that the sinlessness of Jesus is essential to Christian doctrine and does not contradict his true humanity. Quite the opposite, in fact. It is because he was true man that he was sinless. Note that he was sinless *not* because he had a divine "part" which made sure that the human "part" did not sin. It is not because he was divine that he was sinless, but because of his genuinely true humanity.

The case may be otherwise if we ask whether he knew who he was. It is accepted in Christian theology, that when the eternal Son of God became man, he "emptied" himself of certain of his divine powers. As Saint Paul puts it, he "humbled himself." Now, the question is whether omniscience was one of those attributes of which Christ emptied himself. Indeed, one could ask whether Jesus the man of Nazareth had any of the divine attributes. The problem, of course, is that if Jesus did in fact have these attributes, how could he be fully and completely man—man who is finite and lacks such attributes? On the other hand, if he was also fully God, why should he not have such powers? The point is that whichever way one turns, one encounters logical difficulties. It should be clear, then, that whether or not Jesus knew who he was is not a doctrine essential to the Christian faith. The reputed story of Jesus, the child genius who at age twelve argued with the scribes, does not settle the difficulty.

The third question to consider is whether or not Jesus performed miracles. We are not asking whether or not God is omnipotent. Given Jesus Christ, true God and true man, what are the consequences if one says that he did or did not perform miracles? There is no doubt that the gospels attribute to Jesus the power to do the supernatural. He is said to have healed the sick, calmed the storm, exorcised demons, and turned water into wine. Whether or not Jesus actually did such things, however, is quite another question. The gospels need not be taken as historical source-books; they need not be accepted as completely, literally true. This is not to say that the miracles did not occur; it is to say that the Bible cannot be used as proof that they did occur. Despite those who accept the Bible as totally inerrant, the fact remains that any witness to an event does not guarantee the actual occurrence of that event.

Appeal to Scripture does not necessarily answer a theological question. So much we have learned from chapter three. And from our discussion above of the "emptying" of the Son of God, we have learned also that whether one asserts or denies that Jesus did miracles, one runs into a problem. Inasmuch as he is true God, we might be inclined to believe that he did in fact possess divine power. On the other hand, truly human beings are incapable of performing acts which require divine power. As Jesus is both, what can be said?

Some have argued simply that since God is omnipotent, and since Jesus is God, and since the Bible says so, Jesus did perform miracles. We have tried to show above that the last statement is really not a proof, and that the second statement is countered by the assertion that Jesus was also true man. In chapter six we argued that it may be that God in his omnipotence chooses to *limit* his omnipotence—out of respect for the dignity and freedom of his creation. Others have said that the miracles are a sign and foretaste of the Kingdom of God, which is on the way. To this, however, it can be said that the Kingdom comes apparently not because of miracles, but because of humiliation on a cross. Are miracles, which are exhibitions of overt divine power, compatible with the cross, which is a victory won in suffering? On the other hand, some people believe that Jesus could not have performed miracles because miracles are scientifically impossible. The trouble with this position is that it makes science the norm of what God can or cannot do.

There is a variety of ways to handle the question of miracles. It should be obvious that the issue is problematic and cannot be solved with a totally satisfying answer. Jesus Christ, true God and true man. Did he perform miracles? A good question. Perhaps the least we can say is that within the Christian faith both positive and negative answers to the question are perfectly acceptable. Christian theology must say that the basic question is not whether one believes Jesus did miracles or not, but whether one believes he was true God and true man.

We now come to the second major question about Christ: What did Jesus do for man? The Christian church has emphatically proclaimed that persons are saved through Christ; but if one asks, "How?" the answer is by no means clear. It does indeed seem strange that on so important a question Christians should lack an orthodox answer. The church in council did proclaim as orthodox the view that Jesus Christ was true God and true man. But there has never been a universally accepted position on just how it is that Christ saves man. There have been, however, various theories which attempt to answer this question. As we consider these theories, there are two general problems which we must bear in mind. The work of Christ can be spoken of in the past tense. What did he do? But if this work is to be of more than historical interest, we must also inquire as to how Christ's life and death affect us today. As we said in connection with the doctrine of providence, God is alive and well and active in the world *today*. This means that whatever Jesus did in the years A.D. 1-33 must be viewed in conjunction with what he is doing today. Who was Jesus? also means Who *is* Jesus? And What did he do? also means What *is* he doing? The two tenses must be distinguished but cannot be separated. What, then, did Jesus do, and how is it affecting us today?

One theory is that Jesus is our example. He was a good man, a perfect man, and we are to follow in his footsteps. This particular point of view is the one most easily understood and is probably quite widespread among Christians today. The problem is that if

Jesus is *only* an example and nothing more, then certain other points of basic Christian doctrine are denied. First of all, this example theory has no need or desire to claim that Christ was also true God. Secondly, it presupposes that man has the power to live rightly if only he is given a valid guide. But as we saw in connection with our discussion of man, man is a sinful being. And the essence of this sin, according to the Christian faith, is that man does not on his own have the power to live rightly. In other words, man needs more than an example; he needs to receive the power to follow the example. Because of these criticisms, this first theory is generally rejected by most theologians.

A second theory may be called that of sacrifice. God created man good, but man turned against God. So that now, God is angry with men and his anger needs to be appeased. Consequently, God takes it upon himself to appease his anger by sending his Son, who willingly sacrifices his life for the sake of men. God thereby transforms his wrath into love—because of the sacrifice of Jesus Christ.

This view is strangely primitive to the modern mind; a God who requires sacrifice for his appeasement is not easily reconciled with the picture of God, even as Jesus preached about him The church today would be hard put to explain to modern man that he is saved because Jesus was a sacrifice to an angry God.

A similar but different theory speaks in terms of legal imagery. God created man good; but man sinned. In sinning, man violated the honor of God, a violation which is infinite because God is infinite. Man, of himself, has no way to pay back to God that which is due. Further, because God is a just God, he cannot merely forgive, but must punish. Such punishment, however, would obliterate man. So a savior is needed. Because the debt is infinite, the act of the Savior must have infinite worth, the Savior must be no less than God himself. On the other hand, if justice is to be served, man must pay the debt, since it is man who incurred the guilt. The Savior must, therefore, also be man. God, therefore, sends his Son, who is true God and true man in one person.

Christ delivers himself to be crucified, even though he is absolutely innocent. A man of infinite worth is therefore punished with death. As a reward, God owes His Son an infinite favor. And, of course, out of love for man, the Son uses this infinite treasury of merit which he has secured and transfers this merit to those who believe in him.

The argument is apparently neat in its logic and does not violate the other basic doctrines. The sin of man is recognized and the divinity of Christ is necessitated. The two questions of what Jesus did for man and how this affects us today are quite nicely accounted for. The only question is whether this theory is satisfactorily convincing. Does it appear true, or contrived?

A fourth theory projects the image of a great battle. At war in the universe is God against the forces of evil. Man, by misuse of his freedom, has sold himself into bondage. If man is to be saved, a redeemer must come who will liberate man from the hand of the devil. Jesus is such a savior. His life represents the struggle with Satan, his death is apparent defeat, but the Resurrection is the indication that Satan in fact has been overcome and that Jesus is the victor. The details of the imagery are relatively unimportant. What is significant is the basic theme of battle with Jesus Christ as the winner.

For those inclined to accept the objective status of a devil, this theory may prove satisfactory. The danger present is that this "victor" theme could degenerate into a cosmic dualism which, as we have seen, is incompatible with the doctrine of creation. For those who refuse to believe in a devil, the theory has obvious shortcomings. To imagine some sort of a wrestling match between Christ and Satan may be entertaining but is not exactly a persuasive account of what Christ did for man.

In addition to the example, sacrifice, legal, and victor theories, there is another approach which may prove helpful. Beginning with the victor idea, suppose we make the devil into a symbolic representation of temptation. Man, created free, is tempted to misuse his freedom. In fact he does misuse this freedom—that is, he gives in to temptation. Jesus, however, is different. He, too, is free; he, too, is tempted. As a human being, Jesus is tempted to misuse his freedom and his power for selfish purposes. This temptation is symbolized in the Gospel of Matthew. Jesus struggled, he fought to resist temptation, and he succeeded. He proved victorious. Proceeding on this basis, we can say that Christ today enables men to do likewise. Because Jesus overcame temptation, we today, with his help, are capable of the same. Jesus saves. How? By being fully human in his own being and by enabling man also to be fully human. If this is true, there still remains an unanswered and frustrating question. What is the intrinsic connection between his life and ours? Why did Jesus have to be fully human in order to empower us to be likewise? Why was an Incarnation necessary? This question admits of no easy answer. And yet, to this writer it would seem that, given the full range of theories as to what Christ did and does for man, this last view seems the most promising.

Besides these so-called theories of atonement, there is in Christian thought, especially Calvinism, a picture of Jesus Christ which describes his person and work as that of prophet, priest, and king. As the final prophet, Jesus stands in a long line of persons who through the ages have made known God's will. As the very Son of God Himself, Jesus' word is perfect and he represents the culmination of prophetic tradition. Besides making known the will of God, Jesus is also recognized as the One who reconciles God with sinful man. In this capacity he is the perfect priest. God and man need to be brought together again, and Jesus is just such a mediator. Lastly, as the risen Lord, Jesus Christ is also king. Because he overcame evil on the cross, his victory is won, and he is now working to extend his kingdom among men.

These ideas could also be expressed otherwise. As prophet, Jesus *reveals*, i.e., he teaches about God. As priest, he *reconciles*, i.e., he overcomes the chasm separating man from God. As king, he *redeems*, i.e., he leads man out of sin into new life. These parallel concepts no doubt convey a lot of food for thought. And yet, when one describes Jesus as prophet, priest and king it seems more the language of poetry than theology. You could say that a man is a banker, a father, and a member of the Country Club, but it still remains unclear as to just who this person is. You could say that your doctor makes you better physically, mentally, and emotionally, but this does not explain just how it is that he does these things. We are still left with the two tantalizing questions: Who is Jesus? and How does he affect me?

In considering the person and work of Christ we have intentionally postponed until now discussion of the Resurrection. That Jesus was raised from the dead is central to the Christian faith, and yet the interpretation of this event has differed widely. What we shall do here is to examine three views of the resurrection, and in connection with each, ask two questions: Did he literally walk out of the tomb? and What is the significance or meaning of the Resurrection?

The first position, that of orthodox Christianity, is perhaps the most widely held. Here it is believed that Jesus was in fact physically raised from the dead, that his body was resurrected, and that he walked out of the tomb. The resurrection means that heaven, so to speak, has been opened up for all those who believe in Christ. He is the "first-fruits" of those who will be resurrected at the last day and who will go to heaven.

A second position, most strongly put forth by the twentieth-century theologian, Rudolf Bultmann, is quite different. For Bultmann, the Resurrection is not at all something that happened to Jesus, but rather an event in the life of his disciples. Jesus was not physically resuscitated; his body did not come again to life. What happened was this: the disciples came to realize that somehow, through Jesus Christ, they were given the possibility of a new life. Instead of fear, anxiety, and hate, they could now live a life of hope, courage, and love, a life grounded in their faith in Jesus Christ. The Resurrection is the rise of this faith in the hearts of the disciples. Even today, when a person realizes this new life in himself, Jesus is again "resurrected." Further, just as Jesus died and stayed dead, so too, there is no heaven in the beyond for his disciples.

A third view has been recently put forth by a current theologian, Jürgen Moltmann, the basic theme of which is as follows. Jesus of Nazareth was physically raised from the dead. This type of event clearly is no common occurrence. In fact, the Resurrection does not really belong in our time—it is a sign and promise of things to come. The resurrected body of Jesus is a body of wholeness, of joy, of completeness. Our age is one of brokenness and sadness—we are not whole. But the Resurrection of Jesus indicates the way that things *will be*. It is a promise of things to come. Even more, it is the beginning, the inauguration of this new age. As we compare the brokenness of our society to this promise of future wholeness, we realize that things are not the way they ought to be and will be. Therefore, we are given the incentive to change our human society, to become involved in the politics of human life with the hope and the assurance that a better day is coming. In sum, the Resurrection of Jesus is the beginning of a new age and a promise that this new age is coming. Therefore, according to Moltmann, we must work in society, with God, to help him bring in this new age. In this view, there is an intrinsic connection between resurrection and constructive social change. It is the political connotations which separate Moltmann from orthodoxy, and it is both the politics and the assertion of a physical resurrection which distinguishes Moltmann from Bultmann.

No doubt there are other ways in which to interpret the Resurrection. The three views presented are both typical and modern, but they are not without their difficulties. Rather than offering a detailed critique of each, let us content ourselves with two comments. One can criticise Bultmann for not having done justice to the Christian faith. There is no doubt that an integral part of the biblical tradition is the promise of a new day, a Kingdom of God which is coming. Bultmann totally ignores this dimension of a future kingdom. On the other hand, the truth of

Bultmann's position must be considered. How many of us believe that Jesus rose from the dead so that we too will be raised from the dead? How many of us believe in God just to "get into heaven"? To put it the other way, how many Christians today would still base their lives on Christ even though they knew there was no afterlife? If our answer to this last question is "not I!", then our faith to begin with is pure selfishness, and that is no faith at all.

Granted the truth of Bultmann's position, we must question whether it is the whole truth. As we said, the promise of a new kingdom is a basic ingredient of the Christian faith, and the Resurrection of Jesus is, in turn, a key ingredient of the coming kingdom. It would seem, therefore, that there is good theological ground for asserting that Jesus rose physically from the dead.

11

WHAT IS A CHRISTIAN?

The subject of this chapter is the "Christian" life. Man, we have said, is created to live a life of love—a life which has become distorted by sin. Providence is God's attempt to redirect human life, to overcome man's sin. Christ in some way is said to have acted so that a new life would be possible for man. The topic we now need to consider is what this new life is all about. What are the dynamics of overcoming sin and living a life of love and responsibility? What is the style of this new life?

The first question we need to ask is this: how does one come to live this new life? Assuming that there is a difference between selfishness and responsibility, we must consider whatever it is that causes the transition. In the history of Christian thought there have been two basic answers to the question, answers which differ radically.

The first answer goes generally like this. Man is created a free, moral being. God has given man certain rules of faith and morality which man should follow. If man refuses to follow this way laid down by God, then man is to blame. If a person intentionally sins, but later is repentant, God will forgive him. But here again, it is the person who must make the decision to repent. God, really, is not involved in any way other than giving man the guidelines to begin with, and forgiving him when he goes astray.

This position sounds quite reasonable. We all like to believe that decisions are ours to make and that we have the ability to make decisions. Thus, we think that if we wanted to do such and such, we could. It is precisely at this point, however, that many Christian theologians object. Representing the second point of view, they reason as follows. Man is created free and good but has misused his freedom. Consequently, he is no longer really free, but is caught in his sinfulness. Trapped in his own little world where he is the center, man is in bondage to sin. In other words, try as he may, man *cannot* love his neighbor in a selfless and responsible manner. As the apostle Paul put it: "The good that I would, I do not." Wanting to love, he finds himself unable. Consequently, man is described as needing God. He needs God not only to tell him *what* to do, not only to forgive him, but also to give him the power actually to live a good life. That is, in order to love, man needs to be empowered by God. All men are in this position. But now an interesting question arises: if all men equally need God's help, how is it that God doesn't give it to all men? We can't say that some people deserve it while others don't, because we have already said that all men are equally sinful. The only alternative is to say that God helps those whom he wants to help, and passes by those whom he does not want to help. Enter double predestination—the idea that God, by some eternal decision, has elected some people to eternal life and others to eternal damnation.

The church has generally felt that each of these answers is inadequate. The first view, that man has the power in himself to love, does not really take account of the totality of man's sinful nature. Man, by himself, cannot love. On the other hand, the second alternative is equally rejected. Not only is double predestination a reprehensible doctrine, but it seems to make man something of a puppet that God controls. What, then, are we to say? In this thing called salvation, or conversion, or ability to love, what does man do and what does God do? Is there some sort of compromise? There is little doubt that many have attempted some sort of a compromise formula which tried to describe how man's efforts and God's efforts work together. It is another question whether these attempts have been successful.

I myself would put the pieces together in the following way, utilizing concrete illustration. Suppose there is an owner of a small business who happens to be very racist. He has a position open for an assistant, and one day a Puerto Rican comes to him and asks for employment. Will he get the job? From a theological perspective, we can say the following. The businessman is held in bondage by his racism. He finds it impossible to relate to people in a nonracist manner. Of his own, he could not react lovingly and responsibly to the Puerto Rican by offering the job. But God, in his providence, is at work here. Seeking to enable all men to live together in love, God is here challenging the racist *through* the challenge of the prospective employee. That is, the call of the man for a job *is* the call of God to the employer to be responsible. God is involved—but the decision must still be made by the man. If he refuses to offer the job, he has freely made a decision to remain in bondage to his racism. If he says, "O.K., the job is yours," then something new happens. A relationship is established between two people which is and becomes genuinely *human*, a relationship of love and responsibility. And it is *through* this relationship that God now enables the persons involved to continue in love. By analysing the matter in this way, both human freedom and divine power are related in a creative manner. The full depth of human sin is recognized, but the awful doctrine of double predestination is avoided.

However one answers this first question, there is a second kind of issue that can be raised with respect to the Christian life. This issue involves a whole series of questions which pertain not to how one begins this life, but to what this life itself actually looks like. What—if anything—is different about a Christian? Is he converted, forgiven, faithful? Does he have some sort of assurance about salvation that everybody else lacks? All these topics are interrelated and can be put together in a variety of combinations. For the sake of clarity, it will be helpful to paint two pictures of the Christian life—two pictures which are quite different in their understanding of what it means to be a Christian. Let's take the more common opinion first. Probably most people have the following idea of what a Christian person is supposed to be.

The Christian's life is rooted in some kind of conversion, meaning quite simply that the life of sin has given way to a life of faith in God. Sometimes conversion takes a long time to happen; sometimes it happens almost spontaneously in some type of religious experience. It is a conscious experience; a person knows whether or not he is converted. Because it is a conscious event, there is a basic degree of certainty and assurance; one knows that God forgives him and, therefore, that he is saved. The direction of this life is away from sin. Conversion itself is the sorrowful awareness of guilt, the awareness that one has sinned, and is also a conscious beginning in the effort to overcome sin. The Christian, therefore, strives to love other people, a love grounded in his faith in God. To be faithful essentially means to believe in God, to accept the fact that God loves and forgives you, and to seek guidance from God in all things. The faithful person belongs to the church, a community of like-minded people, all of whom also believe in God.

Such, in general, is one picture of the Christian life. There may be variations on some points, but the essentials are as outlined. But this is not the only picture. Consider, for example, the following.

There is no religious conversion. There is no awareness of sin, no sorrow, no search for forgiveness from God. There is, instead, a challenge. People in need call upon a person for help. They challenge a person to respond to them in love and care and concern. Often this love requires sacrifice on the part of the person challenged. There is here no conscious assurance that one is, in fact, loving another person. There is only the attempt to love, an attempt made in full awareness that often our motivations are ambiguous. There is also no conscious belief in God. Consequently, there is also no certainty that one is saved. Because there is no faith, there is probably also no belonging to a church. There are none of these things. But there is love, the attempt to love; there is responsibility and the intention to grow in responsibility to other men. Such is the life of the Christian person.

In comparing these two pictures, some will no doubt be inclined to say that the latter does not portray the Christian life, that it is merely the life of a good but not Christian person. The fact that we so closely identified the former as the only description possible, that we have asserted that a Christian must be a conscious convert, that he must have assurance of salvation, that he must believe in God—this is perhaps more due to force of habit than it is to theological reflection. To illustrate the openness of the discussion, let's look at conversion, assurance, and faith.

The scene is a revival meeting. The preacher has made his pitch; he is calling for people to dedicate their lives to Jesus now. You're there, and you haven't been "saved" yet. The pressure is on, but you just can't do it—you just haven't had the experience yet. Are you abnormal, or what?

Obviously, the answer is no. In fact, there are very few churches or theologians who believe that an instantaneous religious conversion is part of the Christian life. The more commonly accepted position is that the movement towards responsible living is a gradual process, that faith and love grow by inches at a time. The idea of a spontaneous conversion is not essential to Christian thought. This does not mean that people's lives cannot change overnight, for that can happen. It does mean that a religious experience is not essential to the Christian life. It is doubtful, indeed, whether most Christians could look back on their life and say: "Yes, *that* was the turning point in my life."

Not only is the process of conversion open to question, so also is the content. Again, it is usually thought that conversion involves a recognition of sin, a repentant, sorrowful attitude, and an asking for forgiveness. But there is another possibility. To be converted means basically to be changed, to be turned around, to strive for something new. Now, if our racist businessman has, through the power of God, given up his racism, may we not say that he is a changed person—even though there was no consciousness of guilt or need for forgiveness? Or take the case of a suicide whose life was filled with despair and meaninglessness, but who now sees that life can become meaningful if it is lived in service to others. Has not this person been turned around, converted? It would seem that the conversion of a person need not at all necessitate a consciousness of sin and guilt. The ways in which people's lives need changing is much more varied than that.

Another scene we can conjure up is that of the "Are you saved, brother?" type. Fundamentalist evangelists are especially big on this question. The assumption is not only that there is a difference between being saved and not being saved, but also that the person can know it. That is, it is presupposed that faith in God is a matter of consciousness about which one can have full certainty and assurance. The question, of course, is whether absolute assurance of this sort actually exists. Is it possible to know and be assured, beyond all doubt, that one really is saved, that one's faith in God really is true faith? Here again, as a sociological observation, it seems that most people today who strive to be Christian are not at all assured absolutely that their faith is true. Indeed, one could ask whether there could ever be perfect certainty about anything, much less God. It would seem that the most we can say is: "I believe that I am faithful. I hope that I am." So the next time someone asks you whether you are saved, you probably have no right to say anything more than: "I hope so." Of course, you could say much more, but that wouldn't be charitable! Does this mean that faith is taken over by doubt? Not at all. But it does mean that doubt is built right into faith. Not that today I believe, tomorrow I doubt, but that every moment in life contains both elements, one inseparable from the other.

Who is there among us fully aware of the intricacies of the subconscious? Modern psychology has indicated that what we think we know about ourselves is merely the tip of the iceberg. Hidden in the dark corners of our mind are unconscious drives and motivations of which we are not aware. How can one be sure that one's belief in God is not motivated by selfish, sinful interest? How can one be assured that love for another is not simply a manifestation of a perverted sadism or masochism? "Are you saved, brother? Don't you *know*?" Well, not really!

This psychological sophistication is represented in the Reformation doctrine of *simil justus et peccator*. According to Luther, man is both sinful and justified at the same time. Luther himself sweat blood in order to stand perfect before God, finally realizing that he didn't have to be perfect, that God loved him just as he was. The "way we are" is a way in which faith and love are *not* perfect—and therefore we can never be sure that we really are loving and faithful persons. Again, let it be said, inasmuch as most of our mental activity lies in the ambiguity of the subconscious, absolute certainty about the purity of one's faith would seem rather self-deceptive.

Let us conclude this chapter with a note on the nature of faith. Faith is commonly identified with belief. To be a faithful person means that one believes in God. Do you believe that God exists? Yes, I do. Then you are a Christian. No. Faith involves much more than belief. Faith means to so trust in God that life takes on new dimensions, namely, the fullest meaning of love and responsibility. Without love for our fellowman, there is no faith in God. It is impossible to be irresponsible and unloving at the same time one is faithful.

An interesting question arises in this connection. Suppose it is true that man of himself cannot overcome his sinfulness. Suppose, however, that we do in fact encounter a person who does live lovingly and responsibly with his neighbor—but who does not believe in God. What are we to say? That this person only *seems* to love and really does not? But if we consider the life of Mahatma Gandhi, what Christian would dare compare his life to that of this great Indian? Rather than casting aspersions upon another, perhaps we ought to entertain the possibility that a person can be faithful even if he does not believe in God. That is, perhaps the true sign of faith is not belief at all, but love. Even

Saint Paul wrote that there are "faith, hope, love, these three; but the greatest of these is love."

It should be obvious by now that there is no one way that the Christian life is supposed to follow. Conversion, belief, assurance—this particular combination represents one of many possible descriptions of the life of responsibility. Whatever else one may say, this much seems essential: the new life is a life of loving one's neighbor. Without this love there is no Christian, no faith.

12

WHAT AM I TO DO?

One day a student walked into my office. This person happened
to be "head resident" of a dormitory, which meant that he was,
so to speak, in charge. He was responsible for the behavior of all
the residents in that it was his job to maintain order and if any of
the rules were broken, he was to report it to the college ad-
ministration. One of the rules was, in fact, being broken, a rule
involving a serious moral principle. His question was: should he
report it? If he did, the students involved would probably be
suspended from school and, in all likelihood, be drafted into the
armed services. If he did not, other students in the dorm would
no doubt become aware of the situation and could be affected. If
the situation became publicly known, he, as head resident, would
probably lose his job, which paid for much of his tuition, thereby
threatening his own education and career. What was he to do?

A girl discovers that she is pregnant. She is in love with the
father, but he is not at all sure whether he is ready to take on the
responsibilities of a wife and family. Besides, their financial
situation is drastically inadequate, and their parents would not be
very understanding, or so they think. Should she tell her parents?
Should she have an abortion? A woman, married twelve years,
one day meets a man, and after a short period of time, falls in
love. She finds herself uneasy in the presence of her husband, and
often grouchy with the children. Life, she realizes, is but a short
journey, and she dreads the thought of losing this new love which
creates for her so much happiness. On the other hand, she feels an

obligation to her husband and children. What is she to do? Call off her new relationship, and try to be content with what she already has? Tell her husband? Take off down the highway with her new man?

These situations are hardly atypical. Everyone reading these words has been in situations where he or she was torn between the alternatives, unable to decide the right way to act. And it seems that no matter how you decide, you lose. The ethics of human decision sometimes make you just want to cry.

Confronted with such ethical agony, how is one to arrive at a course of action? How does one decide what to do? When caught in a behavioral dilemma, we all want the answer—what am I going to do? But behind that question is a prior one: How do I arrive at that answer? What must I take into account? What are the considerations which will lead to an answer? In other words, the two basic questions for the persons mentioned above pertain not only to what they will do, but how they will arrive at that decision. The two questions of ethical analysis, therefore, refer to content and to method.

What a person does, the content of one's act, depends on how one analyzes the situation, that is, the method by which one decides. We need, therefore, to consider the latter question first. A good way to get into the various methods is to consider two of the letters of Saint Paul, Galatians and First Corinthians.

In Galatia many of the early Christians were converts from Judaism. As the church began to grow, other persons wanted to join who were not Jews, but Gentiles. Now the Jewish converts insisted that all male Gentiles wishing to become Christians had to be circumcised according to the Law of Moses. That is, they felt that all Christians should submit to and accept the legal codes outlined in the Old Testament. For our purposes, the insistence on circumcision is not as significant as the fact that the church in Galatia was insisting on full obedience to the Law. Their position can be reduced to the general rule that, when it comes to ethical decisions, one must obey the law. Appropriately, this position can be called legalism. The basic idea is that once you have a set of laws, you can and must fashion your action in accordance with these laws or principles.

We must note, however, that just what those laws are may vary. For the Galatian Christians, the law was the Law of Moses, which was rather clear-cut. But consider our head resident. If his law was to obey the rules of the college, then in legalistic fashion he would have to report the infractions. That is, regardless of whether or not his act ruined the lives of the students involved, what they were doing was against the law, and they would have to be reported. But maybe he lived by a different principle, such as "always watch our for yourself and do what will best benefit you." If this were the law by which he determined his behavior, he might also end up reporting the students just to save his own skin. Notice how two different principles can lead to the same result—in each case he turned in his fellow students. But the principle was different in each case. In other words, legalism means that whatever law has been set up must always be adhered to, regardless of what the content of that law might be. To take an extreme case, a person might have for a basic principle that whatever the law of society is, one ought to do just the opposite. This person is a legalist! His principle—always break the law!

On a superficial level many people today are legalists. How many times have we heard someone talk about the "principles" by which they live? We say "superficial" in order to indicate that perhaps when it gets down to the actualities of an ethical problem people follow their principles less often than they care to admit. Many so-called good Christians are legalistic at least to the extent of accepting the Ten Commandments as absolute law. In this sense they seem to be following an interpretation of the Old Testament which, by and large, holds that the Law represents the will of God, and even God himself.

Paul's letter to the Galatians is an uncompromising attack on legalism. His main theme is that man is justified before God not because he fulfills the law, but because he believes. When it comes to human behavior, the guide, according to Paul, is not law but love. "For freedom Christ has set us free"—free from the confines of law, free to love. In other words, proper ethical action is guided not by law only, especially not by legalism, but by love. There is a danger, Paul admits that. The danger is that this freedom in Christ could be interpreted as meaning that one can do anything one wants. Since we are free from the law, let us eat, drink, be merry, and do as we please!

It was this attitude which Saint Paul encountered in Corinth. Corinth was something of a wild town, having a reputation for moral laxity and licentiousness. Apparently Paul had preached to the Corinthians about the new freedom in Christ—a freedom which the Corinthians were only too ready to accept! Freedom from law, after all, fitted quite nicely into their already-established free way of life. We can well imagine how horrified Saint Paul must have been to discover that his message of freedom was being used as a rationale for total moral irresponsibility.

The situation among the Corinthian Christians seems to have been that of moral anarchism. "All things are lawful, so let me do as I please." Inasmuch as this was an ethic where law played no role whatsoever, it can be called antinomian (from the Greek words *anti*—against, and *nomos*—law). Whether or not total moral anarchism is possible can be debated. What we can say, however, is that the freedom in Christ of which Saint Paul had spoken, was not to be interpreted along the lines of antinomianism. The difference between Saint Paul and Corinth was love.

All things are lawful—on this they agreed. But Paul added, not all things are helpful. "All things are lawful, but not all things build up." Helpful for what? Building up what? Answer: one's neighbor. One is free to do whatever needs doing in order to love, help, and serve the neighbor. That, in essence, is Paul's way of arriving at an ethical decision. Clearly, what one does in love depends entirely on the situation or context within which one finds himself. On this basis, such an ethic has been called "situationalism" and "contextualism."

The tenth chapter of First Corinthians offers an illustration. In Corinth the Christians lived side-by-side with people who worshipped a variety of gods. The meat offered for sale in the markets was often meat that had first been sacrificed or dedicated to these gods. Should a Christian eat such meat? Why, of course! "Eat whatever is sold on the meat market without raising any question on the ground of conscience." If an unbeliever invites me to dinner and sets on the table meat offered to idols, should I eat? Yes, again. But, Paul adds, suppose a weak Christian, one who does not fully understand this freedom in Christ, is sitting beside you and whispers something like: "This is defiled meat. I don't think we better eat it." If this is the case, then you have to worry about not setting a bad example for this less mature Christian. Maybe, for the sake of his faith, you should not eat. All things are lawful, but not all things are helpful. Love for the neighbor is the only qualifying factor.

Nobody today worries about meat offered to gods, but lots of Christians cringe at the thought of imbibing some alcohol, as though it were a violation of their religion. Many are the times when a clergyman, aware of Christian freedom, has been chastised if not kicked out by a more immature congregation horrified at what they considered to be the immoral activity of their pastor. Taking this freedom seriously, suppose such a pastor frequented the local bar in order to make contact with some of the lonely people there. I put this question to a fine elderly lady once, and her response was that she'd do it—but drink milk or soda pop instead. To this her husband rather quickly replied that he figured he could talk a lot better in the bar if he were drinking what everybody else was!

Freedom, total absolute freedom, qualified only by love—this is the contextual ethic of Saint Paul. You mean I can do anything I want? Yes, provided it is done out of faith in God and love for one's neighbor.

A case can be made for all three of these ethical methods being compatible with Christian faith. Antinomianism could be interpreted as asserting irresponsibility, and this is unacceptable. But it could also be read to mean that in every moment God will inspire one to do the right thing. That is, that apart from all law, the Spirit guides one in making a decision. Interpreted in this fashion, antinomianism comes close to the love ethic. The real choice, therefore, is between legalism and contextualism.

Laws and principles offer security and certainty. They tell us what to do and what not. Or do they? Let's say that you are a Christian who accepts the Ten Commandments as a fundamental law by which you guide your behavior. The third law is interpreted by most—incorrectly—as: Go to church on Sunday. But suppose on this particular Sunday your father is dying in a hospital? Take another case. The fifth law says: Do not kill. And yet when it comes time to go to war, will you not volunteer your service in the armed forces? There are, it seems, cases in which it appears that the right thing to do is to break the law. Can that be so? More critically, there are thousands of ethical problems for which the Law seems to offer no help. Remember the girl who discovered her pregnancy. What law can tell her what to do? Or think of President Truman as he contemplated dropping the atom-bomb on Japan. To what law could he turn? There have been attempts in Christian moral theology to work out answers based on laws for any situation that may arise. But are any two situations ever alike?

It seems to this author that the only way, both biblically and practically, to arrive at ethical decisions is through contextual analysis. This does not mean that one has to come up with a decision in a vacuum. There are some very important aspects of the total context which deserve consideration. To begin with, the total context is that of divine providence. All of our actions take place in a world which God created and which he loves. It is a world in which God right now is seeking to lead us on the road to fulfillment. The ultimate context of our behavior, therefore, is divine love and involvement. Next, and we all know this, whatever we do is a risk. Very seldom are we assured that we're doing the right thing. Christian moralists have always told us that if we obey the will of God, we'll have nothing to worry about. But in the name of God, what *is* God's will? Just as we can only hope that we are faithful persons, so too we can only hope that we are doing the loving thing. If we really believe that God is in control, then ultimately our hope is that God will take whatever we do and bring good out of it. If we make a mistake, God is forgiving. Sometimes we get hung up because we feel that the whole situation rests on our shoulders, which it does not. This is not to detract from the seriousness with which we agonize over our problem; but we should be aware that in the final analysis, we are not alone. God is not only with us, but we have around us fellow human beings. As we indicated in chapter three, in times of distress and trouble, we have about us a community of persons who face similar problems, and they are a source of help. This mutual building-up and comfort is one of the marks characteristic of a true Christian community. Love should be our motivation— as best we can understand our motivations at all. To attempt the loving act means that we must take into consideration all factors—the persons involved, the laws of society, the consequences that might be forthcoming. But oftentimes, even after analyzing all of these considerations, we are still puzzled, and we recognize the need for decision. We can only hope that our decision works out well.

Saint Paul has indeed laid out for us a difficult path. It is often assumed that a situational ethic is easy, that it is much harder to have your principles and stick with them. Further reflection may indicate, however, that the freedom to love and do whatever the situation may call for, m ay indeed be a more frightening responsibility.

13

IS THERE ORDER TO LIFE?

Having considered the methods of ethical analysis, we can move on to some thoughts on the content of human behavior. In setting forth guidelines for behavior, Christian ethicists have frequently spoken of three basic questions pertaining to the Christian life: What is the family? How am I to relate to society-at-large? What does it mean to work? These three questions encompass our life, and they are especially poignant today, because as structures of life, the traditional views of marriage, society, and labor seem to be crumbling. In this time of great insecurity what has Christian theology to say?

Beginning with marriage, we can say that the institution of monogamous marriage is being seriously shaken in our society today. If statistics have any relevance, about 40% of all U.S. marriages end in divorce, and the figure is going up. Of all marriages, statistics show that a majority of husbands and wives will at one time or another commit what moralists are wont to call adultery. Extramarital sex is prevalent, and is coming more and more into the open. Premarital sex is practiced by the vast majority of young people today. Lastly, we can add that homosexuality, if not more prevalent, is at least more vocal.

Coupled with the changes in sexual behavior is an alteration in the general function of women in society. Although the bra-burners are in the vast minority, women are increasingly protesting the ways in which they have been exploited by men. Exploitation may seem a harsh word, but when a woman doing the same work as a man earns only two-thirds of his salary, what else can we call it? Among young women today, fewer and fewer find themselves able to accept the role of housewife as fulfilling their human potential. It is not that they don't want to be mothers, but that they reject the role of the nose-wiping, stay-at-home, clean-the-house type of female. No doubt many girls and most older women find the mother-housewife role quite satisfying. The only question is whether the future may not bring some drastic changes.

The traditional, Christian view of the whole matter has been to reinforce the structure which is now beginning to crumble. The key to it all is the basic idea that marriage is ordained by God. A sacrament in the Catholic Church and a ritual in the Protestant, marriage of a man and woman is believed to be an institution of God which is the cornerstone of a stable society. The purpose of marriage is twofold mutual love between a man and a woman, and procreation of the species. Concern for this latter has led the Catholic Church to reject artificial birth control, but the theological question of birth control seems overshadowed today by the larger question of the stability of the family itself. Carrying through the analysis, inasmuch as marriage is ordained by God, it has been identified as the locus of permitted sexual behavior. Thus, extramarital sex has been banned as the sin of adultery, and premarital sex has likewise been banned as loss of virginity. Because it seemed to violate the structures of existence as given by God, homosexuality also has been branded as perverse and sinful.

It is from this perspective that many Christians deplore the permissiveness and moral laxity in society today. If the divorce rate is high, it is because people don't take marriage seriously. If extramarital sex predominates, it is because people lack self-control and discipline. If young people engage in sexual experimentation, it is because their parents are excessively permissive. And so on.

On the other hand, many psychologists and sociologists argue that the breakdown of the traditional norms of sexuality is a positive development. They argue that there is no reason why young people should not discover themselves and others sexually, that this can be a healthy phenomenon which will later prevent many of the sorrows that arise in an unhappy household. It is further argued that it is nonsense to expect that one person can satisfy all of the needs that an individual has, and that the monogamous relationship should be replaced with a plurality of sexual intimacies. Lastly, the question is raised why, if persons find fulfillment in a non-heterosexual relationship, they should be rejected by society as perverts.

These are the facts and the opinions. How is Christian theology to respond? With respect to all of the other questions we have raised in this book, there has been a wealth of tradition upon which to draw for insight. When it comes to these questions concerning human sexuality, however, about the only position generally represented in church tradition is that which we described above. This does not mean, of course, that the traditional answer is therefore the only answer. What it does mean is that Christians of all persuasions are called to think again in a serious way about the implications of the situation in which society finds itself today. The least that can be agreed upon is that human sexuality is good. Man, as created by God, is a sexual creature, and this sexuality is part of a creation which is not only good, but very good. It has only been a perversion of this idea which has somehow identified sexuality with sinfulness. Again, let us repeat, Christian theology recognizes the goodness of sexuality. The problems arise when one attempts to describe those channels within which that sexuality can be humanly expressed.

The second dimension of human life about which Christian ethics has sought to offer advice is that of labor or work. There were and are some trains of thought, especially in the Catholic church, which differentiate two types of labor—a higher and a lower. The higher way is that of the person who devotes himself to the work of God, that is, a priest or a nun. This higher way is seen as requiring greater discipline and poverty, as embodied in certain vows undertaken. Generally, the Protestant position is that all vocations present an opportunity to be a faithful and loving person, that there is no higher or lower type of labor. Thus, whether one is a farmer, a politician, a janitor or a clergyman, it makes no difference, for all vocations are equal.

Throughout the whole tradition it is agreed that work is a good thing, that man is to be persistent in his labor, and reap the rewards thereof. There can be little doubt that this work ethic pervades the minds of Christians today—a person ought to work! Hence the hostility to persons on welfare. And yet, advances in industrial and agricultural production raise for us today some very serious questions. Our traditional notion of work implies production of a product. If you don't produce something, or fix something, you're really not working. Artists, playwrights, and even clergymen are thought by many to fall into this nonworking category! But what happens when technological automation puts people out of work? This is already happening now, and despite the struggle of unionized labor to maintain jobs, the trend is irreversible. What will we do in the next century when ten percent of the population may be able to run the farms and factories and supply everyone with the things of life? If work or labor is one of the dimensions of life ordained by God, then it seems that we must work out a new concept of what work is. In an automated welfare society, Christian theology needs to rethink the relationship between man and his labor. One possibility might be to begin to think of labor in terms of service to people. Society today has an overabundance of material goods and a paucity of human trust and peace. Perhaps a person should be paid to walk up and down the street just smiling at people and saying hello! Automation will continue and welfare will grow. We must equip ourselves to accept these changes with a positive attitude. Inasmuch as the "work ethic" has been created by Christian theology, it is time for Christians to think about an alternative.

The final topic to be considered under the content of ethics is the relationship between the Christian and society. Beyond doubt, society as it is, is not the Kingdom of God. American society today is pervaded by fear, hatred, exploitation, and apathy. We are basically a thing-oriented society and we struggle against one another to get these things. We are a society of materialism and competition. The question of the relationship between the Christian and society is really the question of how Christian ideals about love and brotherhood are to exist within a society which is headed in the opposite direction.

There are at least four different views on the problem. One accepts the dichotomy as inescapable. A person has faith and love and hope in his heart and has to make the best of it in the hard, cruel world. Indeed, it can be said that one lives in two worlds—the world of religion in the heart and the world of business, war and racism. The two will never meet—these two realms are tragically and forever separated. The only attitude to have, then, is to be as faithful as one can, maintaining a relationship with God, and to be as "clean" as one can while forced to operate and work in society.

A second alternative has been to work within society in the attempt to change it and make it better. The world is hard and cruel, we know that. But it need not stay this way. The way to change it is to work within it and constantly strive to create conditions of peace and justice and freedom. For example, a person might get into politics, hoping ultimately to become a legislator with the power to make new and better laws. Or a church might establish a boycott against a company which practices racism in hiring employees. In other words, on this model, Christians find faith driving them into social and political action in the search for a new society.

The extreme manifestation of this attitude is that of the revolutionary, a third alternative. Faced with entrenched, corrupted power, Christians around the world believe that the only way to change matters is by revolution, including the use of violence. Especially in the so-called Third World have Christians concluded that their faith in God and their love for mankind necessitates the use of armed resistance.

A fourth alternative is that of withdrawal. There have been times in history when people felt that the only way to deal with a totally corrupt society was to leave it and form a different kind of society. That is, finding it impossible to live a life of love and responsibility within the structures as given, they have physically departed and created their own form of communal existence. Many of the great monastic movements at least began with such motivation, although many of them ultimately became at least as corrupt as the society they left! In the United States today, there are many experiments in communal living, where people are "leaving society" as best they can, and seeking to establish a new type of community where materialism and competition are replaced with a spiritual love for one another. The hope is that others in society will take the cue and follow their example.

All of these positions have their difficulties. It can be questioned whether it is humanly possible for a person to live in two separate realms, and still maintain sanity. More to the point is the fact that if God is working in society to change it for the better, how can a person of faith fail to do likewise? The second alternative is certainly a viable option—the Bible itself is full of prophetic persons who sought to change society from within. The difficulty is that frustration can often lead one to give up. Only when one gets involved in the attempt to change the structure from within does one realize the inertia of a system enervated by the misuse of power. Anyone who has tried to force a corporation to follow fair hiring practices, or tried to elect what one believes to be an honest candidate for public office—only then is one aware of the great difficulty involved.

The position of the revolutionary is not enviable. We in the United States are not in a position where violent revolution is necessary or possible. But what would we do if we lived under a Hitler-like dictator? Would we also resort to violence? The question is not lightly answered. The compatibility of love and killing is a matter which no "outsider" has any real right to judge. But for those in a revolutionary situation, the question does remain.

The attempt to form an alternative society is fraught with double difficulty. In the first place, it is well-nigh impossible to get away totally from society. Modern economics and communication are such that even the most radical attempts at isolation find escape impossible. The second problematic is the necessity to beware lest the new society become as evil as was the old. Unfortunately, the history of intentional communities indicates that they are short-lived. This does not mean, however, that this form of protest is impossible, only difficult.

In summary, we can say that the two basic questions of Christian ethics admit of no easy solution. How do I arrive at a decision? The ways of legalism, antinomianism, and contextualism have been described, and we have argued for the latter. What am I do do? Although the full range of the content of ethical decision has certainly not been discussed, we have looked into the areas of marriage, labor and society. In each case, we have seen how the changes in our culture do and can have an impact on theological analysis. There are no easy answers to the tough questions of life, just as there are no easy answers to the questions of what to believe.

14

WHAT AND WHY IS THE CHURCH?

Having just described the Christian life of responsibility, it is imperative we understand that this life cannot be lived in isolation. Man is just not the kind of animal who can make it without "a little help from his friends." This is especially true when it comes to matters of faith and love: there is a basic need for human fellowship.

Take, for example, the matter of faith. No one is so sure of his faith that he does not need strength and support. Faith in God is encouraged when we deal with other persons who also run this risk of faith. The same is true with respect to man's attempts to love his neighbor. Oftentimes we simply fail. Intentions can be misread, our actions may produce undesired results, and sometimes our concern is just plainly rejected by those whom we would love. In this situation we need to know that there are others who find themselves in the same predicament. Being together in the community of love, we are enabled to carry on, to try ever and again, to live the love we seek to give.

This mutual support and concern is an essential dimension of the Christian church. When a child is born, the joy is shared. When a friend dies, the sorrow is borne by all. If the church means anything at all, it means that the struggle to live a life of love, faith, and hope is a struggle shared—and this fact makes the struggle easier to accept.

This communal dimension of human life is embodied in the concept of "the priesthood of all believers." Unfortunately, this concept is usually misunderstood. It is taken to mean that every man is his own priest, that we can all "go straight to God." This is supposed to be a Protestant corrective to the Catholic idea that we need a priest for a go-between. However, that statement that we are all priests is not meant to be taken as saying that we are all our *own* priests. It means, rather, that we are priests to one another. We are our neighbors' priests. That is, we are to serve, care for, and be concerned about one another for we need one another. It is apparently a theme of the American Way of Life that everybody has to go it on his own. Individualism seems to be engrained in our very way of thinking. This individualism carries over into religion; we think that religion is an affair between myself and God. This attitude, we have tried to indicate, is totally misguided. We are individuals, that is certain. But we live within a community—more than that, we need community. This, again, is especially true when it comes to matters of faith and love.

Having said that we need fellowship, the question of the institutional church is bound to arise. According to traditional Catholic theology (now somewhat altered by Vatican II's emphasis on the church as "The people of God"), the institutional church represents God's presence on earth. The order of the priesthood, culminating in the papacy, is, really, constitutive of the church. The Protestant idea puts the institution in a different perspective. The basic reality is the fellowship of persons, who live together in faith and love. The institution is merely a structure which is supposed to facilitate fellowship. That is, the church organization is not the thing itself, but merely enables the fellowship to exist and to function. It may be true in many cases that the institution tends to become identified as the fellowship, but this is a wrong-headed identification.

This difference in attitude between Catholic and Protestant toward the church is reflected in the different attitudes toward the ordained ministry. In Catholic theology a priest is somehow qualitatively different from the ordinary Christian: "once a priest, always a priest." In Protestant thought, on the other hand, a minister is qualitatively no different from anyone else. It is his function which is unique—to preach the Word and administer the sacraments—and this function is bestowed on certain persons for the sake of order in the church. Theoretically, therefore, when a person no longer serves in this capacity in the church, that person is no longer a minister of the Word. For the Catholic, ordination means a change in one's very being; for the Protestant, merely a change in one's function.

During the time of the Reformation, when the universal church was splitting up, there arose a question as to how one was certain whether this group or that was part of the church or not. A criterion was established which was supposed to enable a person to judge. The criterion was this: the church exists where the Word of God is preached and where the sacraments are duly administered. "Word and sacrament" were taken to be the "signs" of the church. John Calvin added a third norm, that of piety. His point was simply that where the church truly exists, a style of life will emerge which will be characterized by obedience to the will of God. But by and large, among the Protestants, "Word and sacrament" were taken as guaranteeing the presence of the church.

It may be seriously questioned whether the criterion is valid. Many civil rights workers who went south to register black voters in the early 1960's were confronted with an interesting dichotomy. The "churches" that had the Word and sacrament were racist. The persons that had no Word, no sacrament, no liturgy, but who were acting out of love for others—they apparently were not the church. Something seemed wrong. And so a new criterion was and is being ventured. Where is the church? The church is where a community of people is actively involved in living in love and responsibility toward one another and toward their fellow-man. There may be no institution, no worship services, but there is a community of love. Such, it is argued, is the church.

Some theologians feel that in some way something more than love is required, such as belief, worship. But even they recognize that besides its worship activity, the church must be involved in the search for social justice. Somehow it seems plainly incongruous for a church to praise the Lord, preach love, and then ignore the ills of society. It is fast becoming recognized that the church must take a stand on certain issues, that it must join in the struggle for human liberation and dignity and equality.

There is, of course, opposition. Many people, Christian or not, think that, at least in America, the church should not become involved in politics. Their argument rests on the constitutional provision for "separation of church and state." A bit of reflection, however, would indicate that this is a total misreading of our constitution. What is prohibited is that the state should hinder the free exercise of religion, that it should establish one particular religion or that it should prohibit another. There is nothing in the constitution which says that the church must not become involved with the politics of social change. Indeed, if such involvement is a mark of the church, then if the church were *not* involved, it would not be the church.

In describing the church, theology has often presented the idea of a threefold mission. In the first place, the faithful community must speak the Word of God, i.e., preach. If in fact God has done what Christian faith believes God to have done, then it is incumbent upon the church to proclaim these acts of God on behalf of mankind. Verbal communication is, therefore, the first duty of the church. This, however, must be followed by a second task, that of service. Inasmuch as faith manifests itself in love, the church is to serve people in society at large. This service might include traditionally accepted forms, such as supporting orphanages and old folks' homes. It could also be interpreted as requiring the church to be involved in the secular struggles for human freedom, justice, and peace. In such activity the community manifests its love for all man. The third element of Christian mission is that the church practice for itself what it preaches. That is, within the Christian community itself there should be seen that kind of mutual love and service which is supposed to characterize the style of the Christian life. These three dimensions of the church's being are often described under the Greek terms of kerygma (proclamation), diakonia (service), and koinonia (community).

Finally, a word on the sacraments. Strange as it may seem, the sacraments have been a major cause of disunity among Christians. The Roman Catholic Church, on the basis of Scripture and tradition, recognizes seven: baptism, confirmation, ordination (of the priest), confession, marriage, communion (the Lord's Supper, the Eucharist) and extreme unction (administered to the dying). The Protestant church, on the other hand, holding to the position that only that which is explicitly founded on the word of Jesus is a sacrament, recognizes only two: baptism and communion. Jesus is believed to have instituted both: "Go ye, therefore, and make disciples of all nations, baptizing them in the name of the Father, Son, and Holy Spirit." "This is my body, which is given for you."

To say that a certain act is a sacrament is to say that in some way God is uniquely present in that act. The only question is: How? The words of Jesus are believed to be "This is my body and my blood." The little word "is", however, is subject to various interpretations.

The Catholic position is to take the verb literally. The priest has before him bread and wine. He repeats the words of Jesus: "This is my body, . . . " and the bread and wine then become body and blood. Of course, they still look and taste like bread and wine, but their "substance" or essence has been changed. Their essence has been "transubstantiated" from bread and wine to body and blood.

Quite the opposite point of view is represented by most Protestant churches. Here it is pointed out that Jesus said: "This do in remembrance of me." The emphasis is placed, not on a literal presence of Jesus achieved by a miraculous transformation, but a spiritual presence. As Jesus is remembered, he is spiritually present in the minds and hearts of believers. The real, empirical presence of God in the sacrament is denied because it is felt that God is too much "Other" to be "contained" within a piece of finite reality.

Luther represents a third point of view. He believed also that God was "Other," somehow "beyond" the world in which we live. But the essence of the gospel, as he saw it, was that this God did in fact "come down" in Jesus Christ and "enter" our world. God really became man—and this real presence is reenacted in the sacrament of communion. Thus, Luther rejected the idea of a merely spiritual presence. On the other hand, he refused to believe that just because a priest recited a few words Jesus was therefore really present. Instead of a magical formula, it was faith which made Christ present. So that for the person of faith, Christ is *really* present "in, with and under" the elements of bread and wine. This view could be summarized as saying that in the sacrament Christ is *really* present if faith is present.

There are other, less official understandings as well. Some believe, for example, that when persons who love one another partake of a meal together, the Last Supper is reenacted, even though they may be heating ham hocks and black-eyed peas, rather than bread and wine. This concept can be carried outside the realm of the common meal: when loving persons are working together for the sake of the kingdom, then Christ is confessed as present. Thus, for example, picketing a segregated lunchcounter could be seen as sacramental action.

The other sacrament common to all Christians is baptism, and here, no less than with the Lord's Supper, confusion reigns. In some way, and no one is sure just how, baptism is connected with sin. There are at least three ways of relating the two concepts.

If one believes that original sin is a sort of biological inheritance which "taints" the soul, then theologically there ought to be a way to "wash" oneself, so that one starts out "clean." This washing is baptism. Obviously, since baptism works as a sort of supernatural Mr. Clean, one ought to be washed as early in life as possible—namely, as an infant. This biological understanding of human sin explains why many parents have their babies baptized immediately after birth. The fear, of course, is that the child might die before the sin is washed away.

A second interpretation of baptism is that it is for adults. Before sin, including "original sin" (however defined), can be forgiven, one must come to a "decision of faith." That is, before baptism can be effective, one must be truly repentant of sin and want forgiveness. This type of adult baptism is prominent at revival meetings, where one is asked to "step forward" and be baptized.

The problem with the former interpretation rests on the underlying notion of original sin, which we have discussed earlier. The whole picture is mechanical and therefore questionable. The latter type, adult baptism, is also subject to criticism. In the first place, it presupposes that God has already "saved" the person inasmuch as that person already has faith. From this perspective, baptism might be said to be superfluous. From a purely human stance, adult baptism can be very dehumanizing. Picture yourself born and raised in a family and church that holds to the belief that you are not a Christian until you have been converted and baptized. You start out young and await your day. You turn 13, 14, 18, 20 . . . Every Sunday you go to church, but somehow you just don't feel saved. Your parents and pastor start to wonder if you're "one of them." The pressure builds, and you're up-tight. This sequence of events has happened to countless persons, most of whom ultimately leave the scene in order to regain peace of mind. So, although on many counts adult baptism with its conscious awareness appears preferable to mechanical infant baptism, it still can be rather cruel at times.

There is a third option. The infant is believed born into a sinful world. At baptism the community of faith—in the place of the child—asks God's forgiveness for the child, and promises to provide a context within which the child can develop into a loving and responsible person. Just as Jesus acted in our place to make us whole, so the community acts in the place of the child in a vicarious fashion. But the most significant aspect of baptism in this view is not that original sin is "erased", not that one finally is converted, but that a promise is made by the community, a promise to God and child that they will provide a community of faith within which the child can grow.

As indicated earlier, the differing views on communion and baptism have become bones of contention within the organized Christian religion. Why this is so can be seen when it is recognized that the problem involved is the whole "way of salvation," and when people think they have *that* figured out, they hate to give it up!

In summary, faith is not purely individualistic. Man needs community, and in the fellowship of love there is a mutual building-up, a mutual concern and love. As a community, the Christian church may be structured as an institution, or it may not. The important point is that, as the Church of Christ, it is involved in what God is doing in the world. Concretely, this means that besides its worship life, the church must also be involved in the world, joining or initiating the search for justice and dignity.

15

WHAT LIES AHEAD?

Although here considered last, by no means least among the topics of Christian theology is that of the future. The question pertains to the direction of history, whether there is a goal towards which time is moving, a purpose which is guiding the course of events. Nobody can really ignore this question, because the destiny of the universe is the context for our destiny. It does make a difference to us whether the world will end in solar burn-out or in a golden age. Christian theology in particular cannot ignore this problem. If God is really alive and well and active in the world today, what he is doing must have some purpose, some end toward which he strives. If man is to work with God in changing the world for the better, there must be some goal in mind. In this light, we can see that our vision of what the future will bring has a formative influence on how we live now. The way in which we perceive what *will* happen shapes the way in which things *do* happen. A boy wants a new ball and so he saves his money. In part, the hope of having the ball causes him to save. The same is true of the Christian life. The vision of the future shapes the way we live and love in the present.

This impact of the future is not to be taken lightly. It is generally recognized that the so-called middle-age years are times of crisis for many people. While one is young, life is exciting because the future is felt to hold a million-and-one possibilities. Travel the world, bum around the country, become president, marry the greatest person alive—all this and more create in the young mind a yearning to strike out on the path of life. But some time, for many people, comes the realization that where you are is where you will be. You have a family, own a house, have steady employment, and tomorrow will be just like today. In many cases this awareness creates a crisis—"I don't want to stay where I am. I want to grow, and do new things." When hope and excitement about the future dissipate, the meaning of the present moment also becomes more difficult to discover. Probably most students today want to graduate from school, get married, have a good job, and settle down. The only question is: what happens when you get there?

The opposite can also occur. If lack of hope for the future can destroy meaning in my life now, too much "living in the future" can have the same effect. Some people see life as a never-ending ladder, where the only way to live is to constantly get a rung higher—a bigger car, house in a nicer neighborhood, and more, and more. Unfortunately for these people, they are never able to enjoy life in the *now*, for tomorrow never comes.

The relationship of the present and the future is an important one for Christian theology. As in our discussion of the Christian life, it will be helpful if we take a closer look at some different pictures of the future. Having described the various theories, we can then examine some specific issues. The first outlook is an amalgamation of orthodox concepts. Time is definitely going somewhere, but the goal lies beyond history, not in it. Time will pass, some men will have faith in God and others won't; some will be moral, others will not. At some time, known only to God, the end of time will begin. There may be a millenium of trials and tribulations, or there may not. But the day will come when history as we know it will cease. Jesus Christ will return to earth in all his glory. All the dead will be raised up, and a Great Judgment will take place. Those who lacked faith and love will be rejected by God and cast into hell, a place of eternal torment. On the other hand, those who were faithful will be accepted into everlasting heavenly bliss.

These ideas are no doubt assumed by many people to be a necessary part of the Christian faith. Yet this is not the case. There are other options, such as the one which follows.

Although it is true that the lives of individual persons have purpose and direction, world history as such does not. There is no final outcome towards which the universe is heading. Individual lives, however, are a different matter. When a person has faith in God, he is, right now, in relationship to the eternal God. Such a relationship is not possible to all men. It is open only to those who through faith have knowledge of God. This relationship to the eternal God—in the here and now, on earth—this is what is meant by eternal life. "Eternal" here is not understood as "forever and ever", but as "related to God." Just as there is no goal to history, there is no life after death. Death is final. Faith in God allows one to accept this finality of death without fear. As there is no afterlife, there is no heaven or hell. Judgment does not occur sometime in the future, but occurs here and now, while we are alive.

There is a third vision of the future which is different still. History is here seen as definitely headed somewhere, and the goal in sight is that of the Kingdom of God on earth. The biblical promise of "a new earth" is taken literally. With God's help, Christ-like people work to change society into a model of perfection. With a basically optimistic view about human capacity and goodness, the hope is that heaven will be established on this earth. History is seen as progressing toward this goal. Not only is time going by, it is a process of improvement. Things are getting better; the Kingdom of God is being ever more closely approximated. The role of judgment and the place of resurrection is not a significant question here. The main characteristic of this view is that it believes the Kingdom will come on earth.

We have, before us, three quite different visions of the future, all of them put forward by Christian theology. As one might guess, no one of them is perfectly adequate. The first option offers no incentive to work towards the Kingdom of God. There is no basic hope that things *will* be better on this earth. The second option, which denies a purpose to world history, is really contrary to much of the biblical witness. An essential aspect of biblical thought is that God has indeed promised a future day, a day when "the lion shall lie down with the lamb." To deny the promise and the hope for a future Kingdom seems to do an injustice to this basic motif in biblical thought. The problem with the third view is that it is perhaps too optimistic. History does not seem to progress; things do not appear to become increasingly better. Faith in the goodness of man and the progress of history is shattered by the realities of war, disaster, and destruction.

Faced with these alternatives and their inadequacies, a fourth position has been suggested. Beginning with the basic premise that God has promised a New Day, it is held that hope for this day is the basic ingredient in Christian faith. The resurrection of Jesus is also the beginning of the end. It is the inauguration of the coming New Age. But Christians cannot just sit around and wait for that day to come. They are called to work with God in helping to bring that day about, helping God fulfill his promise. Man can see that things *are* not the way they *will be*. Therefore, we are called to change the present inhumanities in society. There is an intrinsic connection between the Kingdom of God and the church's involvement in political and social change. It is further held here that *all* men will be included in the promised future. But the distinguishing mark of this position is that God's promise for the future leads to the political involvement of the church. In distinction from the first option, this view contains a definite incentive to change society for the better. In contrast to the second option, it does full justice to the biblical promises of a future Kingdom of God. And in contrast to the third, it recognizes that man is capable of good only with God's help, and that history will not progress by itself, but that it is only through God's providential activity that the Kingdom will come.

Comparing and contrasting these positions in this way illustrates some basic questions which have to do with the future of man. One of these questions has to do with a future, general resurrection from the dead. We usually assume that this idea is basic to Christian faith. But if we listen to some modern theologians, perhaps we should keep an open mind on this question. Someone is here bound to say well, if there is no heaven, why be a Christian? Why go to all the trouble of loving my neighbor if there is no reward? Most people who speak in this way don't really realize what they're saying. It is quite easy to point out to them that if they are Christian just to get into heaven, then they are acting out of the most selfish of motives, and are not really Christian at all. As has been said, the promise of the Kingdom is indeed an essential part of biblical faith. But we should also note that the early Hebrews had no concept of a life after death, and yet they in no way gave up their faith in God.

If we choose to speak of a future resurrection from the dead, we must distinguish this from the idea of an immortal soul. Although it is empirically true that many Christians believe in a soul, it can be said that the concept of an immortal soul is alien to biblical thought. A soul is believed to be immortal, a "part" of man which is indestructible, which never dies. According to the Christian faith, man is a finite creature. There is nothing immortal about man. When he dies, he dies completely. Just as God once created man out of nothing, so again, if God raises man from the dead, man is re-created out of nothing. To say that God re-creates man is quite different from saying that the soul is immortal. We should pay more attention to our Creeds. They speak not of the immortality of the soul, but of the "resurrection of the body."

The idea of resurrection must also be distinguished from that of reincarnation. Belief in reincarnation is the belief that an individual has a succession of lives to live, that when one dies one "comes back" in the form of some other living organism. If one has lived a bad life, one may be reincarnated at a lower level of existence, e.g., as a dog, turtle, or flea. Similarly, if one has been good, one can hope to come back at a higher level, perhaps as a person of great power or great wisdom. In some religions the highest stage to be attained is that of "enlightenment," where a person becomes one with the divine. At that point, bliss is achieved, and the cycle of reincarnation ceases. Resurrection from the dead stands contrary to this belief in reincarnation. According to the former, a person has but one life to live, and then he dies. At some future day, God again brings to life the lifeless. Earthly existence in this view is a one-time affair.

A second question of general interest pertains to the Judgment. Who will participate in the Kingdom of God? Everybody, or just a select few? Both answers have been offered. On the one hand, it is argued that man is given a choice—to love and have faith, or not—and he is held accountable for that choice. If man fails to love, he will be rejected by God. On the other hand, it is argued that God's love for man encompasses even those who reject it. God desires that all men participate in his Kingdom and God's will shall not be thwarted. The difference between faithful and unfaithful persons is not that one is accepted and the other rejected, but that, both being accepted, the former is aware of his acceptance and thus can take more joy in living. How one answers this question depends on one's view of grace and free will.

A third and last question to be raised about the future concerns the relationship between history and that which lies beyond history. Assuming that the Kingdom will come, will it come on earth in human time, or after time as we know it has ceased? If we say that the Kingdom is on the other side of the end of time, then why bother to try to work towards it? If perfect humanity is not possible on earth, why bother to try to change society? On the other hand, if we say that the Kingdom will come on earth and that time will never cease, why do we seem to be making no progress toward that goal? Hatred, envy, selfishness—these and other phenomena seem as intense and widespread as ever. How, then, can the Kingdom come to earth? The problem is a very difficult one, and admits of no easy solution. But the answer to this question clearly determines one's outlook on the possibilities of human effort.

What will the future hold in store? The question is not to be shrugged off lightly nor is it to be answered easily. God knows; we do not. Whatever happens, when the end of time comes for us, there is at least one comforting thought. That is that our search will come to an end, and we will no longer need to ask those questions which perplex the mind. Hopefully, there are no theologians in heaven!

POSTSCRIPT

The path has been tortuous. Question upon question has been raised, and the answers suggested have been less than satisfactory. Mature persons no doubt yearn for the days of their youth when life was simple, and a new toy had the magical power of solving life's problems. Age seems to bring with it the curse of confusion, and the more we know the more we realize how little we really do know.

But the way is irreversible; once the threshold has been crossed, there is no turning back. Saint Paul offered his readers solid meat instead of milk, for they were no longer babes. If Christian theology sometimes confuses the mind, it is because life itself is confusing. And yet, the mystery is that out of confusion arises a unique kind of certainty—an assurance that while one may not have all the right answers, at least one is seeking to ask the right questions. Intellectually as well as ethically, we do well to heed the biblical advice to "work out your own salvation in fear and trembling."

WHAT TO BELIEVE?

THE QUESTIONS OF CHRISTIAN FAITH
by CARL E. KRIEG

To believe is to ask.

The faith of Christians, all too often, is approached on the basis of "Here it is, take it or leave it." Frequently, it seems that the mind of the church has been eternally established, that Christians have all the answers and thus need face no more questions. This book seeks primarily to deal with the questions which any thinking person must raise about Christian faith. Here is no flat description of "what Christians believe." Here, rather, is a helpful attempt to grapple with the deep and perennial questions which must be faced by every serious person.

Why do some people believe in God?   Who is Jesus Christ?
How does God make himself known?   What am I to do?
What does creation mean?   Is there order to life?
Is God still alive and well?   What and why is the church?
What is man?   What lies ahead?
What is sin?

Written in everyday language, this book succeeds remarkably in honestly laying bare the nature of Christian faith. It will broaden and deepen both understanding and experience.

CARL E. KRIEG is Assistant Professor of Religion at Thiel College in Greenville, Pennsylvania. He is also the founder of Spring Run Farm in Greenville—a retreat center for students wishing to study the science of human relations.

Cover by Otto Reinhardt

FORTRESS PRESS
Philadelphia, Pennsylvania 19129

1-1085 $3.25